Gurkha Guns

Gurkha Guns

Published by The Conrad Press in the United Kingdom 2020

Tel: +44(0)1227 472 874 www.theconradpress.com info@theconradpress.com

ISBN 978-1-911546-85-6

Copyright © Ganesh Rai, 2020

The moral right of Ganesh Rai to be identified as author of this work has been asserted in accordance with the Copyright, Designs and Patents Act 1988.

All rights reserved.

Gurkha Guns was translated from the Nepali by Suresh Hachekali and edited by Apjase Kanchha, Kangmang Naresh Rai and James Essinger

Note 1: For publication by The Conrad Press, the English of this translation has been designed to depict Ganesh Rai's authentic voice as a Gurkha soldier. - James Essinger, founder and principal of The Conrad Press

Note 2: the names of Falkland Islanders mentioned in this book have been changed to ensure their privacy.

Typesetting and Cover Design by: Charlotte Mouncey, www.bookstyle.co.uk

The Conrad Press logo was designed by Maria Priestley.

Printed and bound in Great Britain by Clays Ltd, Elcograf S.p.A.

Gurkha Guns

the authentic voice of a British
Gurkha soldier who fought in
the Falklands War 1982

Ganesh Rai

War is the end-game.

Simon Weston CBE, injured British Army survivor of
the Falklands War

Real or imagined, the Gurkhas' mystique was their most potent
weapon in the Falklands War. Just before the final attack on
Port Stanley, the British leaked the plans for a Gurkha invasion.
To the man, the defending Argentines fled, rather than learn
first-hand if the Gurkha legends were more fiction than fact.

TV documentary

To all the Gurkha soldiers who have never
returned home from wars.

Contents

Preface - by the author 11

Chapter 1: Patrolling the Belize-Guatemala Border 19

Chapter 2: Returning to the UK and preparing for going to war 37

Chapter 3: Departing for the battlefield 46

Chapter 4: Embracing war 60

Chapter 5: Here come the Gurkhas! 66

Chapter 6: Confronting the enemy 77

Chapter 7: The attack on Mount Tumbledown 90

Chapter 8: The raging war 104

Chapter 9: The defence of North Arm 123

Chapter 10: Returning to the UK and life afterwards 138

Epilogue: the Victory Parade 163

Preface - by the author

I was born in Nepal, on November 18 1961.

One September evening in 1978, when I was sixteen years old, and having passed my high school exams and eagerly waiting to enrol for pursuing higher education in college level, an Area Recruiting Officer (ARO) came to my remote home. The ARO was accompanied by my father, who was an Area Welfare Officer (AWO): that is a retired British Gurkha army officer who works for the support and welfare of all Gurkha soldiers.

They were heading to Chisapani, a small village where potential recruits were to assemble for Hill Selection the next day.

The ARO, Honorary Captain (Queen's Gurkha Officer) Man bahadur Limbu had been known to me ever since I was a student at Gurkha Army Children School at British Ghopa Camp Dharan where my father was also an ARO. ARO Man bahadur Limbu asked me about my studies and future plans then advised and encouraged me to follow in my father's footstep. I wasn't very keen at first, however, I made up my mind overnight. As a Gurkha, I was of course very conscious of the illustrious military tradition of my people. For Gurkhas, the alternative to being a soldier would typically be becoming a farmer, earning a steady but frankly probably meagre living from the land.

So that was how I joined the British Army at British Gurkhas Depot Dharan, Eastern Nepal, the following year. After successfully completing rigorous Recruit training at Training Depot at Sek kong Hong Kong, I joined my regiment at Gallipoli Lines Hong Kong.

Becoming a Gurkha soldier, I found life totally different from what I had been through as a simple village boy. I trained hard, and travelled to many parts of the globe. In the spring of 1981, my regiment came to UK for a two years tour when, my company was assigned to the duty of protecting Belize against Guatemala's aggression. A war broke out in the Falklands (Malvinas) when we were defending Belize and my regiment the First Battalion, 7th DEO Gurkha Rifles got involved in the Falklands War. A young and immature soldier of twenty years of age, I fought in the war and gained lot of experience.

Having served the British Crown for sixteen years and worked at different levels, I volunteered for early retirement, holding the rank of Warrant Officer Class II. With loads of fond memories and some bitter experiences of my military career, in 1995, I returned to Nepal, where I stayed for next three years. During this stay, I opened and ran a guest house in the capital, Kathmandu.

After retirement, I was looking for a second career abroad and there came an opportunity so, in 1998, I returned to Hong Kong to work in a security sector. After working in Hong Kong for eight years, I moved to the UK with my family. Since then, I have been in employment again in the security field with various security companies.

Currently I am employed as a customer service officer in a prestigious global company, Deloitte, where I meet and greet their clients with, I hope, a true Gurkha courtesy.

The term 'Gurkhas' applies to soldiers who are of Nepalese nationality and ethnic Nepalis of Indian nationality recruited for military forces such as the British Army, Nepalese Army,

Indian Army, United Nations peacekeeping forces and in other war zones around the world.

The word Gurkha derives from that of a medieval Hindu warrior-saint Guru Gorakhnath, who has a historic shrine in the Gorkha district in Nepal. The word itself most likely stems from the Nepali word go-raksh, which is connected etymologically with rakhawala, meaning 'protector.'

Today, there are Gurkha military units in the Nepalese, British and Indian armies enlisted in Nepal, UK and India, and also in Singapore Police and in the French Foreign Legion.

Gurkhas are closely associated with the kukri, a forward-curving Nepali knife, and have a reputation for fearless military prowess. Former Indian Army Chief of Staff Field Marshal Sam Manekshaw once remarked:

If a man says he is not afraid of dying,
he is either lying or he is a Gurkha.

During the Anglo-Nepalese War - which lasted from 1814 to 1816 - between the Gorkha Kingdom (the present-day Federal Democratic Republic of Nepal) and the East India company - the courage and ferocity of the Gorkhali soldiers made a powerful impression on the British, who called them Gurkhas.

The Anglo-Nepalese war was fought between the Gurkha Kingdom of Nepal and the British East India Company. A British political agent named William Fraser was among the first to recognise the potential of Gurkha soldiers in British service and to suggest that the adversaries could be formidable and valuable allies. Subsequently the British proposed forming them into a battalion. This regiment, which later became the 1st King George's Own Gurkha Rifles.

Ever since then, Gurkha forces have been a vital part of the British Army. It is arguable that the role of Gurkha soldiers was no less important than that of British soldiers to establish the British Empire and protect Britain. Gurkhas and their bravery are well renowned in the world.

Sir Ralph Turner, who served with the 2nd Battalion, 3rd Queen Alexandra's Own Gurkha Rifles in the British Indian Army during World War I, wrote the following:

Bravest of the brave, most generous of the generous, never had a country more faithful friends than you [Gurkhas].

Sir Ralph appreciated the Gurkhas because he found them utterly reliable, completely honest and unflaggingly loyal.

Gurkha soldiers fought many wars for the British Empire throughout the world. Many Gurkhas suffered and sacrificed their lives during the war. Gurkha courage, bravery and loyalty towards duty always remained outstandingly high. They always fulfilled their duty with unique courage and bravery both in war and peace.

When Argentina invaded the Falklands, which the Argentines called the Malvinas, on Friday April 2 1982, its government hoped to bolster its support at a time of economic crisis by reclaiming sovereignty of the Islands. In course of fighting many wars for the British, we Gurkha soldiers were deployed to the Falklands to fight the war against the Argentines.

During the war to recapture the Falklands, I fought for the British in the 1st Battalion Seventh Duke of Edinburgh's own Gurkha Rifles. While the Falklands conflict was not officially a war, as Britain never declared war on Argentina nor vice versa, in practice it was one of the most ferocious wars ever fought. In freezing weather and the bleakest and harshest of environments, we fought like tigers.

Gurkhas are great fighters, but like all true warriors they ideally prefer peace. They are sensitive, thoughtful, easily hurt and the image that is sometimes and perniciously perpetrated about them: that they are merely deadly single-minded fighters only obsessed with victory and killing the enemy is totally unreasonable and absolutely unfair.

True, their allies have sometimes found promoting this idea to be a useful propaganda devices and it was applied in the Falklands conflict with the intention of helping to win the war by frightening the Argentinians. Certainly, this strategy was effective: there was a rumour that the Argentine Head of the Government wrote to Nepal government pleading not to send Gurkha soldiers to combat against them since they harboured no hostility with Nepal. Admittedly there is no authentic proof whether the letters of such nature were written but such rumours were heard at that time both in Nepal and Britain.

Whenever war would break out, the British Foreign Office habitually wrote an application to the monarch of Nepal for requesting to grant permission to involve Gurkhas in the battle. The same process was followed in the case of the Falklands war. When the British Ministry of Defence (MOD) issued a notice that a Gurkha battalion was being dispatched to the Falklands as part of the British Task Force, the then British Prime Minister Margaret Thatcher inquired why only one being dispatched. Her question is quite enough to clarify the significance and bravery of the Gurkhas.

At the start of the Second World War, the British Foreign Office wrote an application to Rana of Nepal seeking permission to involve Gurkhas in the war. In response, Rana replied, 'Yes of course you may involve Gurkha soldiers. We are your friends. If you win that will be our victory and if you get defeated that will be our defeat as well.'

Throughout the Falklands war, we Gurkhas fought with the utmost bravery and loyalty following the international rules of war.

Unfortunately, soon after the war, false news started to be spread. Articles were written and published blaming Gurkha soldiers of committing war crimes in the Falklands. They accused the honest Gurkhas of violating the basic norms of human rights. Such mercenary intellectuals through their writing cultivated accusations of the most serious nature such as that the Gurkhas under the influence of intoxicating drugs killed each other, slaughtered their own co-warriors and after the war was over they even beheaded their enemies.

In terms of humanity, nobody has to teach the Gurkhas how to treat Prisoners of Wars (POW) humanely and how to obey international humanitarian law. We know what and how rules are to be followed in the war and how to treat war prisoners humanly and lawfully. We acquired sufficient knowledge and experiences that was needed during and after the wars. We always followed the laws of war and human rights laws in the war. History has shown the truth about Gurkhas. We don't want to have the need of false writers speak for us rather we are capable enough to write our own true history.

This book, *Gurkha Guns*, is one of those histories, and it relates what happened to me, privately, during and in the aftermath, of a huge and momentous international military event, which cost the lives of 255 British soldiers and 649 Argentinian soldiers, and led to 775 British soldiers and 1,657 Argentinian soldiers being wounded. Everyone who fought was extremely brave and willing, whatever their scruples, to lay down their life for their cause. I hope the issue of British sovereignty over the Falklands Islands has now been resolved, and that blood will never more be shed on those islands.

Ganesh Rai, London, November 2019

Chapter 1: Patrolling the Belize-Guatemala Border

Friday April 2 1982

While observing the border between Belize and Guatemala, throughout the day, I was busy with the fighting patrol along with the section commander and other co-warriors. After returning to the camp I was taking a rest in Tree Top Defensive Position, where shelters and trenches were dug.

Suddenly I heard the BBC news broadcast from the VHF 320 radio set, that was a little further in the platoon Headquarters trench (a pit equal to a person's height made for protection from the enemy). I listened very carefully. My attention was drawn towards the news just like the way a butterfly gathers towards the burning lamp. The news said: 'Argentine troops have attacked and invaded the Falklands which was under British rule. Moreover, Argentine troops have captured the Falklands.'

I was shocked to hear this breaking news. Additionally, my surprise was intensified by the news that the British troops were defeated. It was, in fact, the first time in my life I had heard that a country named the Falkland Islands even existed.

After a while, I listened to more of the news of an A351 radio set. The radio operator hurriedly called the platoon commander as though something serious had happened. The platoon commander was WO2 (Warrant Officer) Mani Prasad Rai who communicated the message received from Headquarters to the platoon. As he explained: 'We have received a message that Argentina attacked the Falklands and British marine has been captured. A preparation for war is going on in order to recapture the Falklands. After initial preparations are complete, a British Task Force will make its way to the Falklands with the aim to recapture the islands.'

It had just been two and half years that I was recruited in the British Army. Though I had learnt war skills, I didn't have enough knowledge and experience about war. So, the possible effects of war didn't affect me as much as it was anticipated. Perhaps I was not much worried about the prospects of a Falklands war and its intensity because I didn't get any information of our immediate involvement to join the war. Possibly, I didn't feel anything extraordinary as I was being already involved in an undeclared war against Guatemala. Therefore, I took the news of the Falklands war in a normal and pretty calm way.

The BBC repeatedly broadcast the news of the Argentine attack on two dozen of British Marine Corps and how the Falklands had been captured. The Argentine had been taken the troops as prisoners of war. At that time, my young heart started beating fast with a load of questions: Where is the Falklands Island? How long would the battle go on for? Shall we receive the order to go to the battle, too? Or, should we fight another war here in Belize if Guatemala attacks us? In my heart, I had always realised that the ultimate fate of a soldier was, very possibly, either to kill or be killed.

Monday April 5 1982

We soon got more news: the British had sent a Task Force with a plan to free the Falklands from the clutch of Argentina. In the jungle, we heard the news that the second and the 3rd Battalion Parachute regiments, Marine and Commando Troops equipped with fighter jets, aircraft carriers, frigates, destroyers and submarines being part of the Task Force set off in the mission by ships towards the Southern Atlantic Ocean.

Furthermore, it was announced that the second group of the Task Force, along with necessary armaments, would be dispatched to the Falklands very soon in order to defeat the Argentine troop. Even in that difficult situation, I easily guessed a very major war was going to take place in the Falklands.

Five Infantry Brigade was declared to be the second Task Force. The moment when Five Infantry Brigade was ordered to involve in the war in the second group, we were still closely observing Guatemalan troops by staying in the Tree Top Observation Post which is an observation post made with the bunker in the high ground in the middle dense forest. This latest news created a commotion among us. It felt like a tremor of an earthquake.

Our regiment, 1st Battalion, Seven Gurkha Rifles, was in the UK under Five Infantry Brigade except B Company. We B Company were dispatched to Belize for six months long as part of the Royal Irish Regiment. We had been assigned to fight a possible war against Guatemala, but we were feeling less worried that war in Guatemala would happen as the situation was improving. My heart grew impatient to hear the news of when we would have to set off the Falklands for battle. I thought the possibility of war in Belize would not happen but that my life would be definitely at high risk in the Falklands.

Belize, a central American country, was well known by the name of British Honduras before its independence from Britain. It is a small developing nation located in the west from the Caribbean Sea, in the east from Guatemala and south from Mexico. Remaining as a British colony for a long time, Belize finally became independent on 21 September 1981. Despite its freedom from British colonial rule the possibility of war was highly likely since Guatemala, a neighbouring country of Belize, hadn't given up its claim over Belize. Guatemala claimed its sovereignty over Belize as Guatemala viewed Belize as its territorial part. Moreover, its old stance was continued that Belize shouldn't be granted independence.

The British desire, which was as clear as crystal, was that Guatemala shouldn't capture the weak nation of Belize through military mobilisation. So, the entire security of Belize depended upon Britain. Therefore, British troops had constantly been guarding Belize since 1972.

That's the background to how two companies of the 1st Battalion, Seven Gurkha Rifles, each company having had a six-month tour, were dispatched to Belize under Royal Irish Regiment. From April to October 1981, D Company took the responsibility for the defence of Belize followed by B Company until the war broke out in the Falklands.

I was one among 115 Gurkha soldiers and fifteen British soldiers dispatched to Belize to fight a possible war. Salamanca, which was our base camp, was situated deep inside the jungle. The camp had a capacity to accommodate approximately an entire company of soldiers. It was connected to other military camps by road only, nearest being Rediou camp, Airport camp and the farthest of all being Holdfast camp. Punta Gorda town was the closest town which was almost two hours drive away from Salamanca camp. Most of the country's territory was covered with dense jungle.

The main task of the British troops was to protect Belize from Guatemala's aggression by patrolling along the border of Guatemala. Patrolling along the border through dense forest was our routine task and our priority was to observe enemy activities remaining with utmost alert in observation post. However, the major task of B Company indeed was to guard Belize Guatemala border at the observation post called Tree Top and to face the possible enemy attack remaining in the defensive trenches

Our Tree Top OP location was amidst dense forest, was close to inaccessible and extremely isolated. The site was deprived of transportation facilities and to reach there from Salamanca, we had to use either military helicopters or go up to the half way point by military vehicle and make the rest of journey on foot which would take around three hours. According to the duty schedule, each of the three platoons had to carry out the responsibility of tree top border surveillance in rotation and the duty was extremely nightmarish. One had to be alerted all the time to face enemy's possible attack on the Tree Top Observation Post which was an undeclared war zone literally under the shadow of death.

There was a small settlement consisting of barely twenty to twenty five makeshift sheds across the border in Guatemala, that was connected with other settlements by a dusty road. There was no proper border other than a small stream, which separated Belize from Guatemala. The stream was a lifeline for the local Guatemalans, as they desperately depended upon the stream for their drinking water. Women and girls would come to fetch their water and wash their clothes. The Guatemalan military was not stationed in and around this settlement, but we had to keep on observing every movement made by the local people.

The Guatemalan military, equipped with small arms, would visit time and again in the settlement and border in trucks. We used to be alerted thinking that they might launch an attack. Our suspicion grew thinking that whether they came for border surveillance or for making some strategy. We would inform the platoon Headquarter of their each and every activity through radio set and record every detail on the log book as well.

During the Belize operational tour, Four Platoon, which I was associated with, took the responsibility of border surveillance many times and returned every time to the base camp accomplishing its mission. Due to the dense forest and the field of view being abnormally narrowed down, border patrolling would pose high risk. No alternative was available in this type of situation, except doing everything with caution. Getting more alert, we had to move ahead.

We faced considerable language barriers. The rural farmers wouldn't speak as much English as people from other parts would speak. Under such circumstances, I and some of my colleagues realised the urgent need of learning the local Spanish language.

Meanwhile, an interpreter was appointed for us: a soldier appointed from the local Belize Defence Force (BDF) and he was supposed to accompany us to Tree Top operational tour. But he was very lazy and always reluctant to go out on patrolling. We decided to ask him, to teach us Spanish. As an incentive, we began to offer him chocolates and biscuits that we were given in the periodically distributed ration. This plan worked and soon we were able to speak very basic Spanish.

Otherwise, life on patrol in Belize was not much fun. We were tired, feeling bored and stressed due to the constant patrolling of border area. Then out of the blue we heard that we were to be granted a week's leave, in Honduras.

After a long wait to be freed from this horrible jungle environment even just for a week, we couldn't wait to go to Honduras for our holiday tour. The pace of us learning Spanish increased!

When we got off the plane in Belize City Airport, the temperature was very hot. Air Honduras took off on time for a short journey. After half an hour the aeroplane landed on the hill-surrounded San Pedro Sula Airport. After going through immigration, we took a taxi towards Hotel Tereza, located in the downtown. For a week we enjoyed the urban amenities, visited beautiful places and roamed around shopping centres. It was a wonderful change after our Spartan life in the jungle.

There was a medium-sized park, located in the middle of the city, named American Park. There, every evening, a number of cultural dances were performed. One evening, I went there with my numbary, Dilli Raj. (Numbary is an honorific term to denote a fellow Gurkhas recruit and means that Dilli Raj and I were recruited together). A big crowd of onlookers had gathered in the centre of the park. Just like us, two beautiful girls too were engrossed to view the performance. What is the point of learning Spanish language if it is not used at the right time?

'Sinorita! What a beautiful dance, isn't it?' I was just trying to find out a context to start the conversation with the girls standing next to me and my numbary.

Our conversation continued as I anticipated. Throughout my stay in San Pedro Sula, I would never omit to carry a simple Spanish-language book with me. It would help me extend conversation when needed. The dialogue between two Nepalese youngsters and two Honduran beauties heightened cordiality. Perhaps, our hearts and minds matched. Walking through the street we entered a disco hall. We drank a few pints of beer and we started to dance without stopping. We continuously danced until our whole body sweated. We fully enjoyed at the Disco. The Spanish language learnt in the jungle flourished and of course, the book proved to be just like the twinkling star in the dark in Honduras.

These Honduran beauties were very frank. One day Ek Bahadur and I entered into a restaurant for lunch. We didn't properly understand the menu. A waitress came to take our order. As we had a little knowledge of the food available in that restaurant, we asked the waitress to help with the menu. She guided us about the items. After a while, she came to us to serve the lunch. I guessed she would move away after serving the food but she didn't stir at all.

'Where are you from?' she frankly started to speak to us.

'From Belize. Why?'

'You could speak Spanish if you were from Belize.' I suppose her logic was not incorrect.

We said we were from Nepal and she talked to us for a while. We discovered that her name was Wendy. Our talks continued in friendly manner. In course of our conversation, she said, 'Please, come here to have your dinner, too.'

We didn't have any reason to ignore Wendy's invitation. While paying the bill, she introduced us to her friend. Then we parted and took a cab, which took us to a beauty spot, that was situated in the hill from where the entire scene of the town could be seen.

We joined them for dinner. Wendy did warmly welcome us as though we were familiar for years. Drinking beer, we talked for a while. As the customer increased, Wendy busied herself in their service. It was approaching to be late night so we took our meal. Now, she was free as most of the customers had left and came to chat with us. This time, not only she came, but she also brought her friend with her. Our conversation resumed and at one stage of our conversation, Wendy, suddenly asked Ek Bahadur: 'How about getting married and staying here?'

I was in total shock and surprised by hearing Wendy's courage and one sided decision. So did my pal Ek Bahadur. We had never imagined even in our wildest dreams, that somebody would ask one of us to get married with and stay with her in this unfamiliar part of the world. With full surprises in our minds, we parted around midnight.

It was nearing to be midday, the next day, the telephone of my room rang up. I answered the phone.

'Hi, Mr. Rai! Two lovely ladies want to see you at the reception, please.' It was a female voice from the reception desk.

Astonished, before descending to the reception, I rang Ek Bahadur. Down I went, Wendy and Daisy seen seating in the waiting lobby. They were in the hotel to see us during afternoon break. These lovely girls were not going to let us slip away.

Having lived for a week at San Pedro Sula, in Honduras, lempira (the local currency) was almost finished. We had only a few pennies left. We had to get back to Belize and the jungle that was impatiently waiting for our return.

We had almost had an hour chitchat with afternoon tea and pangs, (a type of local round bread) then Wendy and Daisy went back to where they were from. As they were parting we exchanged our 'hastala vista.'

We returned to Belize carrying a host of resplendent reminiscences. We touched down at Belize City Airport and there was a connection fight back to Punta Gorda. As we arrived back at the airport just like departure there was nothing; no airport staff, no baggage handlers or passport control, nothing at all. We collected our bags and boarded a Four Ton Army Vehicle. Having travelled for two hours in dusty road at last, we reached Salamanca camp showered with dust. However, the hangover of Honduras were still lively and pinching.

We didn't see the girls again but we never forgot them.

Saturday April 10 1982

'Man, you don't understand how difficult it is to take part in a war,' Rifleman Uttarman Limbu, who was going to be a pensioner soon, said, 'Do you know that going to the battlefield very possibly means going there to die?'

'Who cares? We will kill the enemies and wear Victoria Cross on the chest,' stubborn Dipak replied.

'We are in Belize so we won't be sent to the Falklands,' numbary Dilli Raj said.

'If the war goes on, no matter where you based, Gurkhas not only from Belize, but also from Hong Kong and Brunei too, will be called for war, isn't that so, guruji?' Amritman Rai presented his logic after quickly looking at me.

We were arguing amid the swirl of suspicion. In the meantime, the section commander rejoined the section completing his O group at platoon Headquarters.

'An order has been issued that we should go to the battlefield,' Corporal Ram said.

'When should we go, guruji?' All of us asked in one voice as if it was rehearsed.

Upon hearing this news, the colour of Uttarman's countenance suddenly changed. Accustomed to crack jokes with no apparent reason very often, Uttarman stopped talking. Dipak, who used to keep teasing Uttarman, stopped teasing him realising his situation. A name list of the pensioners was published but it was withheld due to the war. The fate of many other senior soldiers turned to be similar to that of Uttarman's.

'Next month I am going to retire as a pensioner. I won't go to the war.' Turning his face gloomy Rifleman Tanka Bahadur Limbu, a year senior to Uttarman, insisted on what was seemed not possible.

Nevertheless, in the battalion Routine Order his flight detail was already published and he was scheduled to return to Nepal via Hong Kong after fifteen years long distinguished military service. We also felt somehow different to hear the warning order to participate in the war. Something erupted inside me. Gradually fear grew. I thought I had to pass the ordeal of my warrior life. After all, fighting a war is an integral part of military life… or death.

Thursday April 15 1982

We of Four Platoon handed over the responsibility of the Tree Top Observation Post to another platoon and returned to Salamanca base camp. Salamanca camp was heated by the news of the war. All were curious to know what was happening in the Falklands. I too began to collect information, especially geographical location about the Falkland Islands on the map, that was pasted on the wall in the information room. Oh my goodness! How far away the battlefield actually was! Eight thousand miles away and surrounded by sea water. Three hundred miles from the coast of Argentina. I found out for the very first time, the Falklands was a small island in South Atlantic Ocean. The spectre-like Falklands haunted our hearts.

In order to fulfill my additional curiosity, I read the historical description of the Falkland Islands pasted on the side of the map hung on the wall in the information room. The information contained as the follows: the Falkland Islands, which have been under the sovereignty of the UK since 1833, is inhabited by approximately 1800 people of Scottish and Welsh origin. They almost all think of themselves as British. Earlier than the British developed human settlement in the Falklands, the island was almost desolate. When the human settlement developed in the Falklands, Argentina began to claim that Las Malvinas or the Falklands belonged to it. As a result, the war in the Falklands began.

Now, thousands of warriors similar to me had to fight a battle for a tiny geographical space located in a distant corner of this planet. Many of us feared we would repose on a funeral pyre.

The war news heard on the Tree Top Defensive Post haunted me everywhere.

It kept haunting me at Salamanca Camp, too. I was much worried about my life. A deep sense of self-love sprouted.

'Hey, forty-seven! You are so lucky. You should have been on six month leave at this time but due to your leave has been cancelled and you are now going to the battlefield. Isn't it?'

How could I say 'No' to Lance Corporal Ratan Bahadur guruji's precise comment about the situation I was having.

'Your leave was cancelled to let you earn more pound sterling by the company 2IC (Second in Command).' Insensitively and enviously spoke Corporal Bal kumar Rai, 'You bloody fool, now face enemy's bullet.'

As Corporal Bal kumar spoke a dominating language I lost my temper. But what could a junior soldier like me do to a gigantic figure wearing chevrons on his robust arms?

'Don't speak so cruelly, Corporal guruji,' I tried to defend myself against his sarcastic comment, 'Who knows, someday I might be awarded the Victoria Cross and wear it proudly, on my chest?'

Even though we had to go to the Falklands for the battle, we were constantly working for the security of Belize. Curiosities were constantly bubbling in our war-haunted minds about what was happening in the Falklands. Reasonable were the curiosities as we were going to fight a battle in which life was horribly insecure.

The information system was very poor in the Salamanca camp. Neither television nor radio were available. We didn't have any other alternative than depending on the date expired tabloids available in the company Operation Room from the

United Kingdom. The same news obtained through these papers about the war was updated and circulated in the company and the platoon. Our ears were eagerly erected to comprehend more about the war.

Friday April 23 1982

Three weeks after the Falklands War started, British troops defeating the enemies recaptured the South Georgia, that is located to the east of the mainland of the Falklands.

All ranks of Salamanca camp were called for roll call in Basket Ball Court in order to communicate the message of this most recent victory. All of us attended the company roll call, where, the company commander Major Pearson, very excitedly reported the news of the British victory over Argentina in South Georgia as though he had won the battle himself.

He tried to boost the morale of the troops, saying 'we should maintain the prestige of Gurkhas which is at the hand of around six hundred Gurkhas who are going to the battlefield.' However, there were around 115 of us in Belize.

Upon hearing this news, I thought we could defeat the Argentine enemies if we were sent to the Falklands. I had to develop self-confidence to strengthen my courage. A twinge of aplomb circulated within me like that of a winner soldier in the battle.

In the camp that was located in the middle of the jungle, we would often watch Hindi movies (Bollywood films) in canteen in the evening. We used to watch the same films many times. The films repeatedly watched in the canteen were; Lahuke Do

Ranga acted by Vinod Khanna, Don by Amitav Bachchan, Kudarat of Phiroj Khan and Jinat Aman. Barsat Ki Eak Rat of Amitav and Rakhi was my favourite, I never got fed up with it.

The famous villain, Gabbar Singh's popular character in the film Shole [Flames] would be caricatured by Rifleman Manoj Rai, many times.

'Hey samba, how many people were there?' Manoj would make us laugh by imitating Gabbar Singh's dialogue in Shole verbatim.

When we wanted a rest from Hindi films, the cassette of Match of the Day would be played in the canteen. Also, ever since the outbreak of the war, we would play videos of the Falklands ongoing war situation every evening. Mostly the video would include scenes of the British troops setting off to its destination by ship, their training, and so on. It greatly helped us understand the war situation.

Once the war began, a large map of the Falklands was put on one side of the wall of the Information Room. For the convenience of understanding the map easily, it was marked indicating the location of United Kingdom, Ascension Island, the Falklands and South Georgia respectably.

There was no question of not marking the targeted Argentina. It was marked with the red colour to indicate it as a hostile nation, which was the principal enemy. Other countries were marked with green, We would gather and discussed among us by consulting the map and guess how far the Falklands Island was.

The date-expired newspapers published in England were available in canteen would be treated not only fresh but a source of our information. Those outdated papers would feel fresh because we wouldn't see other newspapers and magazines in Salamanca camp except Parbate (a monthly newspaper for Gurkha soldiers and their families) monthly.

Parbate had begun to be published in Singapore for the British Gurkha soldiers since 1949. Parbate mostly contained love poems, jokes, short fictions and essays written by the soldiers and their family members.

The middle pages are published in Nepali version whereas the rest of the pages contain the news in English about activities within the Brigade of Gurkhas since early eighties. This publication is very popular among Gurkha soldiers and their families.

Sunday May 2 1982

About a month into the war, Argentina had to pay a high price for its aggression. The Argentine warship General Belgrano was entering the Falklands war zone armed with French-built Exocet missiles. As the Belgrano was approaching the war zone, the British nuclear submarine HMS Conqueror, that was fitted with radar received the information of Belgrano's entry into the killing zone. HMS Conqueror silently pursued the ship and finally fired two extremely powerful and fatal torpedoes, that hit General Belgrano. This was in fact the only time so far in warfare that a nuclear submarine has fired a weapon in anger. The General Belgrano sank with heavy loss of life.

The sinking of the Belgrano became a big news story around the world. At the time of its sinking, the ship had contained more than 1000 soldiers; of which 368 soldiers were killed in the attack.

Argentina got traumatised both physically and psychologically through this loss. General Belgrano was the second largest ship among the Argentine fleet. Additionally, it had the capacity to be equipped with atomic weaponry. The entire nation of Argentina stood against the British. The annihilation of Belgrano and agony of killing of sailors was a huge loss and shock for the entire nation and its people. As a result and ironically, the British attack on the Belgrano became a favorable event to the Argentine military ruler Leopoldo Galtieri, as he was badly struggling to win the favour of public support. Now public support was on his side.

Argentina emphatically raised the issue of Belgrano's loss in the United Nations. Javier Perez de Cuellar, the General Secretary of the United Nations, not only expressed anxiety about the human casualties, he took initiative for the talks in such grave issue in the Security Council. Unfortunately, his attempts didn't succeed. Also, the UN negotiation attempts failed.

This news that we got in the Salamanca camp raised our enthusiasm and ardor. The process of entrusting our responsibility to the incoming company, which was to replace us in Salamanca camp, continued. At the same time, our preparation to return to England also hurriedly kept going. In the meantime in Sennybridge training area, Wales, a joint Five Infantry Brigade Exercise was ongoing. This joint exercise was aimed to be Falklands war training under the name of Welsh falcon.

This training conducted prior to the participation in the war was an opportunity to get prepared for war by revision of war skills as well as to establish mutual understanding between different regiments. Unfortunately, due to us being in Belize, we couldn't participate in such an important training. During the Welsh Falcon exercise, a terrible Land Rover accident happened. Sergeant Ran Bahadur Limbu who was travelling with a load full of ammunition, got killed. This was indeed a terrible loss for our battalion. We were all emotionally devastated.

Chapter 2: Returning to the UK and preparing for going to war

Tuesday May 4 1982

When we were about to leave Belize, we heard news reminding us that so much of war is about destruction. After waiting for the right moment for taking revenge for the destruction of the General Belgrano, less than forty-eight hours later, an Argentine Super Entendard fighter bomber, made a counter-attack against the British destroyer HMS Sheffield. The news of the destruction of HMS Sheffield by two enemy Exocet missiles sensationally spread out.

The first missile missed the target, the second missile hit it. The destroyed Sheffield sank into the sea in the chilling cold of the southern Atlantic Ocean. Twenty men were killed; twenty-four were critically wounded.

The news of the destruction of the British warship was, of course, spread joyfully throughout Argentina as a result of this news, with excitement and happiness, Argentines poured into the street for celebration. They exchanged happy shouts, sang, danced and chanted slogans. I thought a very strange and contrast attitude of human beings was on display. How could a human being get delighted in somebody else's killing? On one side, people were mourning, on the other side, delectation.

An Argentine diplomat, living in America responded disparaging his diplomatic discipline and human sentiments. He was glad about the British deaths.

What a resentful sentiment! I thought: it was all a huge loss of life and property just for a small piece of land located in the middle of the sea. Such colossal resentment, enmity, revenge, killing and carnage! In which, very soon, I was going to be involved with.

The war in the Falklands had begun for the sole purpose of establishing rights over the islands between Argentina and Britain. As is well known by now, the war turned out to be brutal and gruesome. The loss of human beings, warships, jet fighters and helicopters increased on both sides.

During the war, British Frigate HMS Ardent and HMS Antelope were also destroyed. In addition to HMS Sheffield, HMS Coventry, a Type 42 (Sheffield-class) destroyer of the Royal Navy also annihilated and the pieces scattered on the seabed. It was practically proven that war is nothing more than ruination.

Loss on the enemy side was similar to that of the British, though about three times as many Argentines were killed. No side was in the mood to compromise. Some were killed at sea and others on the Falklands. At least, some traces were left in the case of those for whom, a palmful of flowers could be offered on the spot where they were fallen. But it was not possible to find trace of those whose lives perished in the sea of water where, heart like candle could be burn for their honour. Either soil or water. Either life or death. There were simply two alternatives, nothing more. The unavoidable truth was that we were getting involved in the bloody war of Falklands.

Saturday May 8 1982

After handing over the responsibilities of the Salamanca sector to the company of a British regiment, we were returning to Punta Gorda in a four-ton army vehicle with the unforgettable memories of Belize in our heart and minds. The wheels of the vehicle were generating clouds of dust as if it was screening the scene behind.

Sweating throughout the day in the parching sun, Punta Gorda was perhaps, taking rest in the shadow as we reached there in the evening. The coconut leaves were moving like the fans by the coastal breeze. I imagined as if Punta Gorda was waving its loving hand of farewell to us and telling us that there is no meaning of your life in the whirl of war. And also probably it was telling us to go to the battlefield as soon as possible as death was waiting.

We left the four-tonner at Punta Gorda and couple of hours later boarded the ship. Being jam-packed throughout the night, like a flock of sheep and goat in RPL - this stands for Ramped Powered Lighter; it's a military landing-craft with the capacity to transport around eighty soldiers - over the Caribbean Sea. The voyage was one of the worst I have ever experienced. We kept jolting and became seasick. We got exhausted in the voyage. We restlessly waited for the morning so that we could free ourselves from the inane journey. Some of us were too exhausted and desperately wanted to disembark, no matter if the journey was complete or not.

After a painful night-long journey, at last in the morning, the journey was over and we disembarked the ship at Belize city port. We were free of troubles finally, but not free of hangovers.

We were transported to the Airport Camp by Army four tonners. As usual, it was another hot day, so two soldiers outside the barrack were sunbathing almost naked, only wearing their underwear. I was inside the room along with some friends. A black cleaner girl was coming towards the barrack. One of the two soldiers sunbathing, called the black girl by showing a magazine, 'Olga, have a look at this magazine.'

'Which magazine is that?' Olga inquired.

I thought it was a football magazine. The girl began to flip the pages of the magazine. Both soldiers began to laugh. 'What happened to you?' The girl concentrated on the magazine. Her black complexion brightened up.

'Johnny, come over.'

One of them waved his hand to call me as if I didn't know English. I was interested to know what the magazine was about. I went there. My face reddened with shyness to see the magazine Olga was flipping through.

The fully mature Olga was not ashamed of it at all. She kept looking at the porn magazine and said to me, 'do you like to read it, too?'

After a round of satisfaction, she put the magazine on my hand. I felt shy and didn't know what to do. The two soldiers began to tease Olga. She wouldn't step back but challenged them, 'Come on.'

While impatiently waiting to board the plane at APC in evening, the images of Tree Top Observation Post haunted my memory. Furthermore, my mind presupposed the possible horrible images of the Falklands war. I observed my own life from various angles of vision. One time I found life like going ahead through the straight line, another time I found it strangely entangled at the turning. I realized about military life: One who walks stumbles, one who doesn't walk doesn't stumble.

In spite of the fact that so many rivulets of feeling overflowed in my bosom, they couldn't crumble down my firm heart though.

While leaving Belize in the dusk, we boarded the same Victoria Cross Ten (VC Ten) Plane, wore the same regimental mufti dress and returned to UK. The only difference I found was, while arriving in Belize, my firm heart was thrived with the golden imagination of Belize, whereas while departing I felt like the death shadow was chasing me every moment.

After almost over two hours of departing Belize, our aeroplane landed at Washington D.C. We stayed at the transit room for well over an hour. Despite, the night outside was dark, we took photos in order to keep our memories alive.

From a bookshop in the airport, I bought Time published in the United States. The magazine, that contained the interviews of the British Prime Minister, Margaret Thatcher and the American President Ronald Reagan about the Falklands war. Moreover, the opinion of the American Secretary of State Alexander Haig also was included. That was the sole reason for me buying this magazine.

During my flight from Washington D.C. to Brize Norton in Oxfordshire in the UK, I somehow managed to finish reading the magazine, but I got next to no sleep.

What I just read had a profound impact on me. I felt myself determined and my spirit lifted up. President Reagan had fully supported the British demand and persistence 'as the Falklands, an inseparable territory of the United Kingdom.' In addition to this he also pointed out that, 'with the initiative of the United Nations, the Argentine troops should immediately step down.' Most importantly, he also had made a pledge to assist the British in the war if required. The weight of the statement of the American President is always regarded heavy in the international world.

Having read the interview, I, a most junior soldier, had my morale boosted, let alone the entire British chain of commands. Winning the favour of the United States was, a massive boost to the self-confidence of the British. The interviews ignited hope within me that the war could be won. I could imagine how tremendous this morale boost was to the higher ranked officials of UK Ministry of Defence.

Sunday May 9 1982

The VC-10 landed at Brize Norton Airport, Oxfordshire, early in the morning. This was the same airport where we, while heading off very early in the morning to Belize six months previously, had stayed overnight. Having had an approximately three-hour long bus journey, we reached Queen Elizabeth Second Barrack, Church Crookham, near Aldershot, Hampshire, the home of the British army.

As soon as we entered the camp through the main gate, I realised the ambience was conveying the pre-signal of war. The barracks seemed lively though the countenance of the soldiers seen walking around the barracks were gloomy.

When we arrived back the UK from Belize, the entire regiment was being fully prepared for the war. They were just waiting for the departing day to board the cruise liner from Southampton and eventually to the battlefield. Delight sprouted in a corner of my heart as if, after a long time away, I just had returned home. When we entered the empty spider-shaped Barracks, it appeared to have lost in oblivion for six months in our absence. These barracks were indeed the home for us soldiers, though the only difference I felt was, in those barracks, no mother was waiting for us with affection. However, I felt cordiality with the rooms in the barrack. My heart gaily smiled at the barracks.

No sooner had we entered the barracks, an order was immediately issued to get ourselves prepared for the war. We had very limited time for battle preparations. In a very short time span of three days, we tried as best as we could to manage every preparation intact.

We did zeroing (an important work of adjusting sights in hitting the target with rifles and machine guns) in the short range that was built inside the camp. We fired our personal weapons just to make sure they worked properly and hit the target.

After preparing the personal weapons we collected warm uniforms for the winter. They included Arctic clothing, new type of bergens (a type of rucksack we use in the army) and pouches, as the ones we had been using were not suitable for the war in the Falklands. As per the list of the paraphernalia to carry in the battlefield like maps, compasses, protectors, binoculars, we packed rapidly. While packing was undergoing, an order was given to pack extra clothes not only in bergens but in the kit bags, too.

We all were physically prepared to go to the war, however, making ourselves mentally prepared was even harder than we ever thought. Psychological terror kept on haunting us. Nobody definitely would smile and step out of door to go to fight the enemy in war. Some senior soldiers, especially those who were about to retire on pension, often had a low opinion of having to fight in the war. They would miserably say, 'I should really be pensioned off, but they didn't let me retire. Now, I have to go to the battlefield.'

In fact, probably no soldier is ever happy about having to the battlefield to fight an enemy. I grew sympathetic towards their plight.

'I won't go to the battle. I am a pensioner. Please release me,' Ran Bahadur Limbu, a senior corporal of my platoon submitted an application to the platoon commander.

The simple and unavoidable fact is that a soldier is recruited to fight a battle and, in the battlefield, the soldier either kills the enemy or gets killed by the enemy. This is the bottom line for all service personnel. Who doesn't love his or her life? Even a beast loves its life let alone a human being. Who would be ready to die in the world? However, being war-bound soldiers, we can never shirk our duty and responsibility.

Every soldier is bound to fulfil the oath they have administered holding the regimental battle honours during attestation parade. Otherwise, the oath, if not fulfilled, might bring misfortune. In the Army, life would mobilise as per the order. A soldier, who is expected not to be afraid of dangers. Orders and soldiers are supplementary to each other like two sides of a single coin.

In course of our orientation about the Falklands war, we were informed about the enemies' condition, uniform, weaponry, tactics, strengths, psychology and many more.

According to the newspaper report, the Falklands war was the consequence of the military dementia of the Argentine military ruler General Leopoldo Galtieri. Argentinian people were pretty fed up with military rule, so they were aggressively against the Junta ruler. General Galtieri had an inner plan to ensconce his weakness and unpopularity and divert people's attention towards the war thereby promoting his popularity through sympathy. In order to achieve this target, he had issued an order to attack the Falklands.

During the orientation, we were told that since in Argentina there was a provision of compulsory military service to the public, most of the soldiers were not regular and experienced or even fully trained. We were efficient professionals, they were mostly maladroit amateurs. All this vital information about enemies boosted our moral. We felt sure we would win.

The news of the Falklands war was all pervasive as if there was not any other subject. The television channels would broadcast news, views and counter-views about the war in a regular basis. In our company information room, we could see the maps of the Falklands, posters of the weapons and current situation of the war attached all over of walls. Newspapers were covered with the photographs and the hot news related to the Falklands.

When we got fully prepared to go to the Falklands and engage in combat, the entire British people became much electrified as if they were also ready to set off the Falklands. The moment the whole Britain was afflicted by the Falklands-phobia, how could only the warriors remain unmoved by the fright of war?

Chapter 3: Departing for the battlefield

Wednesday May 12 1982

As per the movement order issued the previous day, the whole battalion along with the full kit made its presence at the parade square at six o'clock in the morning. In order to carry us to the Southampton Port, on one side of the parade ground, there was a row of the comfortable coaches just like a row of the soldiers.

'21158370 Sergeant Agendra Bahadur Limbu.'

'Present, sir.'

'21161077 Lance Corporal Ratan Bahadur Rai.'

'Yes, Major guruji.'

'21163247 Rifleman Ganesh kumar Rai.'

'Yes, Major sahib.'

There was an early morning roll call by the Company Sergeant Major (CSM). He took the attendance of all the members of the company who were going to the battlefield.

We boarded the coaches after the roll call. The row of warrior-stuffed coaches moved towards the Guardroom. The soldiers residing in barracks in the Queen Elizabeth II Barrack looked desolate in our absence. The camps without soldiers looked like a widow in her early age. The arbitrary, glamour less and bleak camp looked as if it was going to let its tears fall in our farewell.

The civilian staff, who were workers in the camp and the unlucky soldiers, couldn't participate in the war due to various reasons, waved the hands of farewell to us by standing in a row in front of the Guardroom. The troubled time abruptly made me remember my old father. I don't know how my mother would say goodbye to me if she was still alive.

I remember how one day when I was a boy I went to graze the flock of goats in a nearby field from my house with my slightly older village brother named Kale at my village of Hadikhola, Khotang, Nepal.

Forgetting our duty to keep a vigil on the flock of goats, we began to soak our heads splashing water. We were immersed in our business. We didn't notice when my mother came to fetch water. After a while, kale brother saw her and scampered saying 'dema, dema (dema is a respected word to address the person whose husband is older than that of the father of someone.) I didn't move at all rather stood still confidently thinking she wouldn't beat me up.

But unlike my expectation my mother beat me with a stick saying, 'You played with water like an idiot instead of guarding the goats.' Perhaps I wouldn't weep if others had beaten me. But as a pampered child I cried when mother thrashed me. She kept on thrashing me without trying to silence me. I cried at the top of my tongue being wrapped by her gunyue (a garment that was worn by women in the past in the villages of Nepal). The moment she saw the imprint of her stick on my calf, she tried to coax me, 'Don't weep my little prince. Why did you soak your head with water that way? Don't you get sick?'

Mother's coaxing further aggravated me. I wept bitter tears of dejection. My weeping stopped only then, when mother wiped my tears.

This reminiscence made my eyes teary while I boarded the coach.

I couldn't get my mother's love for a long time. My dear mother tragically died when I was just four years old. She passed away just six days after giving birth to my younger brother Mangal, who fortunately survived. We children were all looked after by my grand mother. So I was deprived of motherly love when I was very young. In fact, I can't recall my mother's face. I am so unlucky that I don't even have any image of the wonderful lady who gave me birth.

Once again, I wiped my tears.

Ironically, I was going to the war but none of my family members, who were living thousands of miles away in Nepal, knew about it. What kind of obligation! How treacherous time! My unlucky relatives were unknown about my life that was fallen in crisis.

I grew emotional. Emotionally I let the tears drop. I found my life's circumstances very cruel and awkward. However, I didn't divert from my military responsibilities which made me a diligent soldier heading to the battleground.

From the main gate of the Guardroom to the Fleet town, the local residents were waving their hands standing on the roadside. This farewell was simultaneously creating a mixed feeling of consolation and anxiety. The passengers of buses and cars were waving their hands to bid us goodbyes throughout the motorway until we reached Southampton. Newspapers had published news reports about our departure, so did the television channels broadcast the same news of Five Infantry Brigade being sent to the South Atlantic. Therefore, majority of public were aware of our journey and destination.

The whole week of our departure, newspapers had published the photographs of Gurkha soldiers sharpening their kukris, the famous curved knives we use, and attacking the enemies by holding rifles on their left hand and glistering kukris on right hand on their front pages. The kukri and khukri spellings are of Indian origin the original Nepali form being kukri. Theoretically expert on the significance, influence and use of media, the British editors and publishers waged media war through the print media. However, it was surely not a war like the First World War and the Second World War to be fought with kukris. In first and second world wars, Gurkhas used their kukri to kill the enemies in close combat. Gurkhas are well known for their bravery and for their personal knife, the kukri. Even today, every Gurkha soldier keeps a kukri in their webbing.

When we were about to reach Southampton, a group of people were waving to us through the window from inside a considerably tall and great glasshouse. Probably, it was an office building. Some of them were leaning against the chairs and looking at us. I surmised either a spring of compassion originated for us in their inner heart or they didn't understand any emotional dimension of life or they didn't know anything about warriors' psychology. Nevertheless, we were travelling a war journey in a pitiable condition.

We reached Southampton, the biggest port city in southern Britain. An insuperable crowd of people in the port was ready to bid us a grand farewell. The luxurious gargantuan Queen Elizabeth II Liner was waiting for us in order to take us to the the war-vortex. We were being sent to the Southern Atlantic Ocean in one of the most immense and tremendous cruise liners ever built.

The ship would be being guarded and escorted by destroyer, submarine and frigates towards the war zone.

At our appointed time, we boarded the liner carrying our kit bags, bergens and personal weapons. It was quite natural that the British people who were chanting and were concentrating on us the very moment we were in a queue to board the liner. They looked somehow impatient for us to depart.

Along with the fluttering of flags held on their hands, tears were flooding out of their eyes. The moment was very emotional. People were bidding goodbye to either their husbands or brothers or fathers or boyfriends or relatives or friends. Whose heart remains unaffected in such moment? Who doesn't cry in love of their relatives? This farewell might turn to be the last farewell forever for some of us.

The gloomy faces and tender teardrops falling down the eyes of the goodbye-waving people badly disturbed my heart. My love for life heightened. I realised my life so closely. I got lost within myself in limitless love and reminiscence of my relatives and family in remote villages in Nepal.

Making a long row, as per plan, we embarked the Queen Elizabeth II. We were allocated rooms as soon as we got inside the ship. The room I had been allocated needed to be shared by three of us. My room partners were numbary Dilli Raj Rai, who was recruited together with me, and junior fellow Rifleman Padam Bahadur Limbu. In addition to we Gurkha soldiers, there were the soldiers of the 2nd Battalion, Royal Scots Guard and 1st Battalion, Royal Wales Guard in the liner as well. Among the soldiers on board of more than three thousand, the majority was of infantry men like us. And the rest were soldiers from other trades.

We lined up on the deck of the ship as per the order for final farewell. People were going to see us off and vice versa. On the platform down on the deck, hundreds of people were wriggling like chhichimira: a kind of moth found in Nepal which emerges from the undergrowth in a swarm in the spring season.

THE FALKLANDS ARE OURS
KICK THE ARGENTINES OUT
BRAVE GURKHAS ARE ON THE WAY
GOD BLESS YOU ALL
GOODBYE Task Force

This is how; the feelings and opinions of British people about the Falklands were articulated through banners and placards. Standing on the deck above, I read the opinions as much as possible. And those materials soothed my bruised heart scratched by the fright of war. Individual names along with messages were written in some placards. Those messages were written wishing success and safe return from the battle ground. The swarm of well-wishers prayed that the battle ground bound members of the Task Force could return safe and sound winning the battle.

The port seemed covered with Union Jacks and the regimental flags. There was a huge number of media present to cover our departure and the expectation of British people to free Falklands by us was immense. The army band, that was playing farewell melodies which was changing the ambience into more tragic, woeful and grievous. Almost all present at the port were wiping their teary eyes and were waving us too.

At ten to four in the afternoon, a high-pitched sound echoed round the port to indicate that the ship was about to depart. Queen Elizabeth II set off towards the extremely uncertain war journey, carrying us in its body. We had to cross eight thousand miles through the Atlantic Ocean to reach the Falklands.

The land gradually became invisible. The QE II moved ahead along with the company of birds and whiff of zephyr.

The same evening, I received the letter that my father had sent from home. I got despondent when I went through the letter in which things were written about family matters and about my younger brothers, elder sister and step-mother.

My father had also mentioned that he had a prospective bride for me. I had never seen the girl. She hadn't seen me, either. However, I became sentimental and could imagine the girl's images.

The letter made me thoughtful. I was so anxious throughout the journey. A grave fright grew within me that my would-be wife might be marked as my widow even without getting married, if I got killed in war. I prayed the God thousands of time for the sake of my safety.

I had never boarded a liner as immense and huge as Queen Elizabeth II in my life. There were amenities like a swimming-pool, a post office, a cinema hall, a theatre and even a banking facility inside the liner. There were means of entertainment too, such as night club, dining hall, pub and bar as though the liner was heading towards the Falklands, carrying a whole town.

Both the front and the back of the liner were transformed into helipad.

During the voyage we were given various trainings about infantry skills. As the Sea King helicopter was entirely new for us, we made a repeated drill of getting on and off on the helipad until we were perfect with the drill. Another important thing we learnt during voyage, was reading of the maps of the Falklands. We practised first aid for the treatment of the injured in the war. Under the supervision of medic, we repeatedly did things like bandaging wounds, sealing bullet holes using field dressings and giving morphine to the shocked patients. Time and again, we were given information about the presence of enemies who had captured the Falklands, their condition, their strategy and their confidence level by member of Intelligent Section.

As infantrymen we also did weapons training of course. We practised the skills of stripping and assembling of the rifle, and loading and unloading it, then had to do all this when we were blindfolded. We did practice night rifle handling drills and many more to win the battle.

To keep ourselves fit, we ran for half an hour round the deck of the ship every morning.

Sunday May 16 1982

May 16 is a special and historical day in our regiment because it is our regimental day. 7 Gurkha Rifles was founded at Thyetmyo in Burma on 16 May in 1902. The regiment was raised by Major E Vansittart that had been known as 7 GR (Gurkha Rifles) until 1959. But in 1959, the regiment was awarded the title of Duke of Edinburgh Own Gurkha Rifles. Since then it had been known as 7th Duke of Edinburgh Own Gurkha Rifles or 7th DEO Gurkha Rifles in short.

This year's May 16 was historical and unforgettable for the reason we were moving for the Falklands War. We celebrated Eightieth Birthday of our regiment in the Queen Elizabeth II liner. There was just a simple formality of cake cutting without any sporting events. However, May 16 was turning to be historical and significance because the regiment was on its way to the Falklands. Where the regiment was to fight with utmost courage and dedication and to defeat the enemy then gaining another battle honour.

The whole regiment gathered at a place, where the space was available enough to accommodate all members. Commanding Officer Lieutenant Colonel David Morgan and Gurkha Major Lal Bahadur Rai delivered speeches wishing everyone to fight and liberate the Falklands and to keep the Gurkhas name intact. Then a small cake was cut to formalise the celebration. We each had few cans of beer and soft drinks.

The regimental birthday celebration was the first ever being celebrated in such a grand ship like Queen Elizabeth II. And most probably this will be the last one too.

Having had the drinks, there followed a few rounds of Nepali dancing and singing. As that was the only way of entertainment we could do under such circumstances. A kind of delight and enthusiasm filled all of ours heart. The formation of the psychology that 'the military with high morale can defeat the enemy' was highly positive in the context of fighting a war.

Monday May 17 1982

The platoon commander delivered lectures just like other evenings to update the situational report in the Falklands. After the platoon commander came the platoon Sergeant, who would deliver a talk about the administration aspects of what we were going to be doing. And at last but not least, the section commanders gave us a lecture summing up everything. Possibly, for the purpose of keeping us entertained and free of anxiety, there were films shows in QEII every evening. As the war progressed our minds were made up too. My frightened heart was growing stronger and stronger that whatever be the result; there would be no option other than accepting it. Either death or safe return. Especially, the seniors, who were extremely anxious of their family mostly for their wives and children in Nepal, were looking sad and anxious.

Rifleman Tanka Bahadur Limbu was sitting on the bed in the corner looking melancholy. To boost his morale I said, 'Don't worry, guruji! Do have courage. We won't die in the battle.'

'You can say so because you don't have a wife and children.'

'Do not make your heart weak this way saying you have wife and children?' Trying to convince Rifleman Tanka Bahadur, Lance Corporal Ratan Bahadur said, 'Do you think only you have wife and children? So do I. So others.' Tanka Bahadur's face brightened up a little.

Everybody hopes to live till they survive. Who likes to die untimely? So, in the tough twilight situation of life and death, in order to boost my colleagues' morale up as usual, I said, 'Argentina will never beat the British.' Uttarman got up from the bed and said, 'Are you sure?'

'Sure, Argentina can never win the world-ruling Britain,' Lance Corporal Ratan Bahadur added.

'The British have colonised many powerful nations,' Rifleman Dipak looking at Uttarman, all of a sudden, said, 'Don't you have any idea about this? Yes, the British will win. No doubt of it. But triumph is not achieved in a war without soldiers' sacrifice. Isn't it?' Numbary Dilli Raj opined.

Absolutely right. Victory and defeat are not finalised without fight and death of the soldiers.

My strong conviction was that Britain wouldn't be defeated by Argentina at any cost. I would try to console my fellow comrades that as much as possible the problem would be resolved through negotiations since the United Kingdom is a permanent member nation in the Security Council of the United Nations. I could easily surmise through such logic in the platoon so that my colleagues as well as Uttarman Limbu and Tanka Bahadur Limbu among the seniors would be convinced to a greater extent. Perhaps due to this reason they would frequently like to hear such things from me. Moreover, I wouldn't like to sadden them. Whatever, the level of fear and anxiousness I had inside me, I kept trying my level as best as I could to maintain others' enthusiasm.

Tuesday May 18 1982

Seven days after our departure from Southampton, the liner came to the seashore for a short time. I found out that the seaport where our liner had docked was Freetown, the capital of Sierra Leon, a nation that was once colonised by Great Britain. The ship had only docked for refuelling. We were not permitted to disembark the liner.

Due to the extreme heat, we couldn't stay in the scalding cabin as the liner stopped over for twenty-four hours. We went to the deck upstairs for fresh breeze. It was sweltering there, too, though.

The mail service was still active. Incoming letters were distributed. It was only my father who would write me, I had sent a letter home before leaving Belize and also had sent one just before I set off for war from Church Crookham. I mentioned in the letter that I had deployed in the Falklands war and not to worry about me. There was no question of not sending response to my father's last letter which I received the day I boarded the liner for the war. I had expressed the feeling that troubled me on the pages of paper and sent home. Sending my letter's response so soon from home was impossible. I didn't expect it as well.

My father himself had been a soldier and had fought in the war against Japanese troops in Burma during the Second Word war. Moreover, he was an experienced person fighting a guerrilla war against the communist rebels at Borneo confrontation. Probably, he wouldn't worry much on my current situation. Perhaps, my mother would much too worry if she was still alive. Now, my elder sister would feel anxious and depressed much because she had her husband too, going to war as I was.

Rifleman Tikaram Rai, my brother-in-law, who enlisted two years before me, was in the same regiment as I was. He was in Support Company. My younger brother and younger step-brother were small, unable to know many more things about war. My love somehow grew for the step-mother, too.

Luckily, I had not fallen in the cobweb of marital relation yet. Sorry to say, love alone doesn't sustain the world. We were obligated to fight a terrible battle against foes and secure our own beautiful future.

My older colleagues got seriously disturbed upon reading the letters written by their better-halves. The corner of their eyes grew damp, thinking what if we die then our children wouldn't be able to get the fatherly love and support that they deserve like every other kid. Their children would be helpless because of not money but due to loss of their fathers. Their psychology was difficult to decipher. Despite the fact that penetrating their heart was not possible, their gestures and postures could articulate internal anxiety. Sorrow would be bubbling up throughout their eyes that would attempt to shove me to the ocean of sentiment.

After finishing refueling, Queen Elizabeth II moved ahead from Freetown. During the platoon lecture, we were informed that our liner was heading to Ascension Island another British colony in Atlantic Ocean. As earlier, we started various war trainings in the liner. We had not only to fight the war in the Falklands, we had to win it because life would sustain in victory.

The sweltering heat might be the pre-signal that we had reached very near to the Equator. Everybody looked sweating. In my free time, I would watch the bright sun on the blue sea water. The shoals of dolphin would plunge and leap up in water then move to the direction of the liner. Suppose the shoals of dolphins were following us or they probably said, 'Anything might occur in the war, so better have a view of our performance rather than missing it.'

Ascension Island is an isolated volcanic island, south of the Equator in the South Atlantic Ocean. It is about 4,000 miles from the Falklands and so about half-way between Britain and the Falklands.

We were warned the moment our liner approached around Ascension Island, that we were entering into a perilous area. An order was issued to blackout the liner. Moreover, we were also instructed not to open the window, not to turn unnecessary lights on. Movement on the deck needed to be ceased would mean our chances to feel the fresh oceanic breeze and enjoy the scene ended. From then on, we had to limit ourselves in a tiny cabin that contained sweltering heat.

The Queen Elizabeth II, which transported us to the Falklands battlefield, was originally made for the use of wealthy cruise passengers. It would certainly be a great mistake even to think the liner might have to bear tremendous loss from the foes' attack. It was boarded with more precious warriors than the liner itself.

For this reason, it was obvious that the military-packed liner would be the major target of the opponent. Of course, we had our military escort, but we were still vulnerable.

It was crucial, at any cost, to avoid the attack of Exocet missile launched in the water and safely land the troops at the Falklands. Anyhow, this challenging duty had to be accomplished. Our confidence level was gradually building up which strengthened our inner spirit that helped us in becoming less and less fearful from the anxiety of war as trainings continued.

An aerial attack was going on over the Falklands while we were sailing on the sea. British troops were vigorously making an attempt to land on the Falklands whereas the opponents were making it a failure. As the British naval forces were cordoning off the islands by constant patrolling to ensure the Argentine forces would not get additional troops and armaments and could not resupply extra military force and additional weaponry.

Chapter 4: Embracing war

Friday May 21 1982

Today, three further days into our journey, we heard great news onboard that encouraged us to think the British could win in the Falklands. Despite Argentine's attempt to stop British troops' landing on the Falklands, combined force of about 2,500 of parachute regiment, marines and commandos eventually succeeded gaining footholds in Port San Carlos. During this beach head landing, there was an intense fighting.

The landing of the British troops on San Carlos for the first time after Argentina captured the Falklands, became an important news for the BBC to broadcast repeatedly as if the news was the only and the ultimate weapon to win the war. This news raised our morale. Our countenance brightened up. Some of the soldiers gathered in the canteen and celebrated. We got delighted, too. War-on-the-land would be more secured than war-on-the-sea. To defeat the foes on land, one has to land on the ground too so there were multiple advantages of the San Carlos Beach Head landing rather than disadvantages.

No matter how much aerial attack is made, unless the infantry gets directly involved to the battlefield and confront the enemies, victory can't be assured. Therefore, this beachhead landing on San Carlos was absolutely significant to recapture the Falklands. That is why, we soldiers' inner spirit lifted in hearing this successful landing.

The hot weather gradually cooled down as much as the QE II sailed on towards the South Atlantic Ocean. The cloudless bright days began to look overcast. The pattern of oceanic waves began to change. Mailing services ceased to exist. But training continued without stoppage. Live firing practice on the sea began from the liner's deck. Nobody knows how many innocent aquatic creatures were killed by so many bullets that more than 2000 soldiers of three infantry battalions fired.

In course of the voyage, we were told; the QE II would take us only a far as South Georgia. For the onward journey from South Georgia to the Falklands we'd have to go with other ships.

The more the QE II headed towards South Georgia, the colder the weather became. We felt the necessity of arctic clothing when we were assigned the duty of defending the ship from enemy's aerial attack. We got posted on the open deck with machine guns.

As we were closing in to South Georgia, we required to shift from QE II to the ship that would take us to Falklands. To accomplish this mission, time and again, we practiced the way of moving from one liner to another safely on board. The dry drill of ups and downs on the ship's floors with full kits and paraphernalia made us enormously sweating even in such cold. Strict orders were issued to carry personnel weapons such as rifles and machine guns with ammunition. To put on the helmet during movement was also ordered. As we were on the way to battlefield, the circumstances we were in the moment, made us feel the way as if we already got to the battleground. War was intensifying in the Falklands so did we escalating practice after practice about the war in the QE II.

Friday May 28 1982

After ten days of leaving the vaporous land of Free Town, we reached South Georgia which was covered in snow. There were even icebergs here and there in the sea.

South Georgia had already been recaptured. There was no fighting persisted in South Georgia, that was how QE II safely managed to voyage troops up to the island. There were two medium-sized passengers ships I saw in the sea through the rounded window of the cabin I shared with colleagues. I guessed those liners were there being readied to transport us to the Falklands.

Just before our arrival at South Georgia, platoon order was issued to us to board the liner named Canberra. But it was not so. Suddenly, another behest followed instantly to board the next liner named Norland. Perhaps the plan was changed due to the change in war-strategy. As per our dry training to shift from one liner to another we changed the ship without any hassle.

On leaving the QE II, we expressed gratitude to the crews who dispatched us to South Georgia in a long trip safe and sound. The crews of the liner, standing on a row bade us goodbye. They emboldened us through a round of applause and wished a success in our mission. Finally, they sailed back to the UK.

Following the timetable, we, the 1st Battalion, Seven Gurkha Rifles boarded Norland whereas the 2nd Battalion, Scots Guards and the 1st Battalion, Wales Guards boarded the Canberra, a bit bigger liner than Norland. Cabins were given to us. As soon as we had our cabins, the crews of the liner informed us about the safety required to be followed.

The duty of defending the Norland began just like on the QE II. Machine guns were posted out on the deck in severe cold weather. Despite the extreme weather conditions, we carried out the responsibility being utmost alert. Fighting the enemies was tough so did the cold. However, there did not fly any enemy's fighters over our sky.

Saturday May 29 1982

At midnight, both Canberra and Norland made their voyages to fight the Argentines. Of course, the closer we got to the Falklands, the higher the security threat was. Warning was given to be cautious because the threat of aerial attack was very high and it might take place any moment. Except those bound to anti-aircraft duty, others were prohibited to go up to the deck. We repeatedly took the training of getting under the bed at the soonest after wearing a helmet provided an aerial attack takes place while staying in the cabin. I thought then, in fact, we were fallen in the vortex of death. We had to find the way to survive. As the saying sprung through my mind: when there is a will there is a way. I was trying to find the way to survive by all means at any cost.

On the voyage to the Falklands, we had to endure a great deal of suffering. The ocean became very choppy. And the weather became extreme cold with high wind. During the platoon lecture, in the evening, the platoon commander updated us about the ongoing battle. The update was; Parachute regiments had defeated the Argentine forces in Goose Green and Darwin.

The news of the Goose Green and Darwin victory was just like a huge lift that energised our spirit. And the victory expanded the wave of enthusiasm among us. It also ignited our determination that the turn of victory over enemies was ours. Meanwhile, we heard a tragic news that in course of Goose Green attack the Commanding Officer of Two Parachute Regiment, Lieutenant Colonel Herbert Jones had been fallen. As much as I was joyous about hearing the news of the victory, I was desperately sad to hear of the Commanding Officer's death.

We didn't know how many soldiers were killed from either side in the Goose Green Battle. We were also not said how many were injured, rather we got the news in great number of enemies were killed. And many of them were made prisoners of war by the Paras. This news served a great excitement on the journey to the battle.

Sunday May 30 1982

When we reached the vicinity of the Falklands, oceanic rollers tormented us in a crazy way. Rollers began to rise over rollers almost to turn the liner upside down. The sea didn't remain blue, quiet and adoring at all. Both the sea and the firmament turned black. We had to face the extremely terrible natural environment. As a signal of Stand To (a state of readiness for counter-attack at any moment of high probability of enemies' attack) siren produced high-pitched sound. The moment that I accursed to thrust myself under the bed carrying a rifle under my arms, I thought the missile bomb would be going to destroy Norland.

We were obliged to thrust under the bed in our cabins until stood down.

War was naturally challenging in the water. The moment we were intoxicated with sea sickness and silently cursed the enemy, then said: we would make the enemy understand how fatal war was provided we could go ashore. We might get buried in the pit of death. Perhaps we had forgotten ourselves.

Many of us got seasick onboard Norland which violently shook with the rollers and almost turned over the ship. Luckily, I didn't get too sick. Committed to kill the enemies in the war, we were likely to die with the symptoms like getting dizzy, vomiting and anorexia. There is a saying that Gurkhas are not good sailors. It proved so especially in Norland. Many co-warriors began to look tenebrous and gloomy for which they were regularly upchucking. They looked nervous one-sided and did barf wherever gone. The impasse inside the liner was like their vomit would make sick to the well-conditioned, too. Perhaps it was the result of being the citizen of a land-locked country like Nepal. Many of us were sick, including me,

Ultimately, winning over the adverse challenges of nature and avoiding the enemies' eyes, on 31 May, the last night of the month, Norland stopped at Beach Head near the port of San Carlos. Besieging the Falklands within the circumference of 200 miles, British warships were bombarding the enemies. We remained inside Norland waiting for an appropriate moment to disembark on the land. My heart was pounding and just wishing to get down the ship to securely step ashore.

Chapter 5: Here come the Gurkhas!

Tuesday June 1 1982

It was not an easy task to disembark from the Norland, that was still some miles away from the shore. The enemy's threat was very high as bombs were blasting and firing was going on. It was all violent and frightening, but we were highly-trained Gurkha soldiers and used to this and indeed we had expected it. Throughout the night, we were trained how to disembark securely and quickly and shift over to an RPL from Norland. As efficient as in training, in the dawn on 1 June, we shifted over to RPL from Norland without being spotted by enemy.

The RPL, full of soldiers, speedily sailed towards the shore. The objective was to securely shift the warriors to the shore from Norland without any loss. After getting to the seashore we boarded off the RPL at the soonest.

Eventually, for the first time, Gurkha footsteps trod on the Falklands soil.

While disembarking we didn't get to face the enemy's assault. Perhaps the enemy didn't have any clue about our landing in San Carlos.

My body was accustomed to shake as for twenty-one days the liner constantly shook in our voyage. So, I felt as if my body was shaking on the land, too. However, the reunion with the land after three long weeks, emboldened me. I thought, now, I wouldn't die in the war. Anyhow, I will return alive in the place where I was born and grown up.

In the San Carlos area, which was surrounded by gentle hills, some of the British soldiers were found busied themselves on anti-aircraft duty. Machine guns fixed to poles were pointing towards the sky. They played a great role on our landing. After a while, the area got filled with warriors. We dug trenches in the damp ground. We stayed in the trenches, but remained fully alert. After spending around two hours in San Carlos, each company was assigned to its tasks. B Company's task was to secure Goose Green, which had been recaptured from the enemy most recently after a fierce fight.

A Chinook helicopter flew us towards our destination and rest of the companies were also flown for their task. I had only seen Chinook before but never boarded on it. Therefore, it was exciting experience to me just like the ongoing war. The helicopter didn't directly fly us to land us at Goose Green, instead we landed at Darwin, a tiny hamlet, that was few kilometers apart from Goose Green.

The scene at Darwin was pretty terrifying. The captured Argentine POWs, who wore green khakis with no weapons, were carrying the corpses of their co-warriors in tractor and dumping in pit. Perhaps they were burying the dead bodies. Yet I didn't have much time to sway in the swing of sentiment. And also, I was not deployed on the battlefield to judge humanity. Despite the ongoing sentiment, I controlled myself and concentrated on the game of the war.

Carrying a heavy bergen, that was almost half of my height, on my back, my weapons on extreme alert and spare magazines and ammunitions in pouches we moved ahead to Goose Green. The path we had been following was sludgy. Most of

Goose Green is often sodden with brackish water; this naturally makes the going very difficult. On the sludgy path our journey continuously moved ahead in the darkness until we reached Goose Green.

It was a dismal midnight when we reached Goose Green. We spent the first night in the open field.

Wednesday June 2 1982

Early in the morning, we saw what Goose Green really looks like. Located on the coast and containing around thirty to forty houses, Goose Green, in spite of being beautiful, due to the war looked pitiable losing its beauty. For the first time we saw few residents of Goose Green. Looking at their innocent eyes I deduced they were not free from the fright of war, yet. The residents of this settlement who witnessed the plight of war few days ago, were looked like to us Gurkhas in term of the height. Neither very tall nor too short, just an average height like ours, they looked florid, brown complexioned and amicable.

Those among us close to the house, leaned against the walls of the local houses in early morning chill, seemed to be lucky as few of them got served with morning teas and coffees by some inhabitants. And I was one of them got a hot mug of coffee. In the chilling cold of the morning their cordiality was more than enough. In our very brief conversation they narrated unlimited misbehaviours of Argentine soldiers.

'We had to remain within the four walls of house in a curfew as coming and going was prohibited. The Argentine troops would steal food we were taking into our houses and if we didn't surrender they would show weapons and try to manhandle the women,' While chatting and serving me coffee a gentleman said, 'They snatched our motor-vehicle, too.'

The same gentleman also told me that they heard Gurkhas were coming but they had never seen them. The arrival of the British troops had somewhat consoled them. However, a deep anxiety still ruled over them that another retreat might take place.

The aftermath of war was present throughout Goose Green. There were motor vehicles bombed-out recently, anti-aircraft gun and the dilapidated remains of the fighter planes were scattered everywhere on the area. We were told that large number of prisoners of war had been kept in large hangers which looked like built for keeping sheep. As we moved out of Goose Green, there were things like ammunitions for rifles, rounds filled magazines, belts of bullets for machine guns lying all over the ground. Defensive trenches dug around human settlements by Argentinians looked forlorn. Perhaps those were the trenches from where Argentine troops had defended and tried to launch counter attacks against the British onslaught.

B Company was ordered to protect Goose Green from the possible enemy attack. So, following the footsteps of section commander we moved to the upper part of the territory that was slightly raised and suitable from defensive prospect.

We constantly worked for the defence of Goose Green. No matter whether it was day or night, we dug trenches almost our height deep. We carried out anti aircraft duty on a rotation basis throughout the day. During night, we manned the Sentry Post in pairs to keep monitoring enemy activities. The adverse weather posed difficulty. It was not only cold but windy too, that prohibited us from listening to the enemy activities. The Machine Gun and the Rifles in the sentry posts were made ready to discharge bullets at any time.

Thursday June 3 1982

The weather in the Falklands was very variable and frankly usually pretty terrible. My home country Nepal is quite poor and has many problems, but at least it has a very warm climate, which is more than you can say about the Falklands.

There, in a very short interval of time there would be rainfall, snowfall and wind blow. We raised walls out of clod of earth around the trenches in order to protect ourselves from such adverse weather. Besides this, we made shade out of the zinc sheets in order to keep the trench dry from rainfall.

The Falklands climate was extremely peculiar too. The darkness, I meant the night was fifteen hours long whereas the day was only nine hours. Sunlight was very rare like praying to a god but not receiving his grace of presence. During the war period, I realised the day was more comfortable and cordial despite the fact that sunlight was absent.

Our anxiety would not much elevate due to the activities during day but at night, with the darkness, it was difficult for our hearts not to fill with terror. Our psyche would turn one-sided when we did sentry duty with machine gun and rifle in pairs. Nothing was visible in the pitch darkness. Wind would let nothing hear. Heart would get more terrified as things would look only in murky shape while scanning through the Individual Weapon Site. At night, sheep would look like human figures heading towards us like kneeling down. To fire the bullet just in guess was not permissible. We wished night never encircled Goose Green. Though the rule of nature would never change howbeit we wished.

According to the company's defensive plan to defend Goose Green, we, members of One Section, were out front in the forward position taking the responsibility of the Forward Section within the platoon. Two Section was on the right-hand side, platoon Headquarter in the middle and the Three Section was on reserve at the rear of the defence. Enemy's air threat was imminent. Therefore, if there was any aircraft flying over, we had to carry out stand to and ready to fire the weapons to shoot the fighter.

We had been ordered, in the case of air threat, to be stood to so on hearing the aircraft flying over, we would immediately stand to and ready to fire the weapons. Every day, we had to stay in ready position several times to bring down the fighter with a shot. However, the fighter didn't dare fly over our firmament even a single time. Very few flew but they were our Harrier Fighters flown for mission. Fighting patrol, reconnaissance patrol and clearance patrol were carried out continuously as they were routine tasks to be done when remaining in a defensive position.

Five Platoon, on the command of Lieutenant (QGO) Bhuwani Shanker Rai, was on our left hand side just about 500 meter away from us. They were on an elevated land as we were. Lieutenant (QGO) Garjaman Gurung who was commanding Six Platoon during Falklands war and his platoon was on the low and slightly hidden terrain in depth position. And the company Headquarter obviously was in the middle of the platoons to command the platoons more efficiently. Our company commander, Captain Lester Holy had recently come from Special Air Services. He joined the company immediately after our arrival from Belize. He was not like other company commanders as he couldn't speak Gurkhali (Nepali) language at all and was new in the battalion. Moreover, it was his first experience to work with Gurkhas. During the war, communication was not possible between him and the lower rank soldiers. But he was very pragmatic and would always get involved on nitty-gritty of soldiers' problems. He was also very serious about soldiers' welfare. His action was enough to fulfil the lack of linguistic gap. He gradually became familiar with Gurkha kaida, the tradition and habitual style of Gurkhas in the battlefield.

Fighting was going on in other parts of the Falklands. Mainly Second and Third Battalion of Parachute regiments, Royal Marines and Commando Forces were taking part in the fightings. We, First Battalion, Seventh DEO Gurkha Rifles, along with our co-warriors of Second Battalion, Scots Guards and First Battalion, Welsh Guards were in various location in defending the Falklands waiting for the order of invasion.

Monday June 7 1982

While in the defensive position, from the intelligence source a notice was issued to us that there was an enemy appearance quite some distance from our location.

A fighting patrol needed to be dispatched to the area where the enemies were sighted, so the platoon commander, Warrant Officer Mani Prasad Rai gave an order for fighting patrol to us (One Section) in order to defeat the enemies. After the section commander Corporal Ram Bahadur Gurung gave detail order for fighting patrol, the Land Rover took us to the drop off point through tactical driving in darkness.

The moment we were getting off the Land Rover, suddenly we heard human voices. There may not be other people except enemies in the desolate land at that night. We got into all round defence at once to shoot and kill the enemies. My heartbeat increased uncontrollably and it kept on so with a great anxiety of either killing the enemies or merely being killed by them. We tried our best to listen to the enemies' movement and the noises they would make with utmost alert thinking either we will kill, or we will be killed. My index finger was already inside the trigger guard and the safety catch was also off, ready to press the trigger. The Machine Gunner Purna Bahadur Rai, who was beside me, was ready too, just like me, to fire the gimpy (military slang for general-purpose machine gun or GPMG). We observed the foes' movement in silence, but nothing was heard. The wind let us hear nothing except the briefly repeated rush of wind. But we tried to listen to it.

Now, we had to move ahead in search of enemies. Nobody got up. We were stuck on the damp ground. Scout one had to get up first to lead the movement and then Scout Two. And then, according to the section formation, the section commander had to lead the whole section. At the furthest back of the section, I, section 2IC (Second In Command) had to follow the section taking the responsibility of a gun controller. I didn't get up first since I shouldn't have to. Obliged to get up first, the Scout One also hadn't gotten up. The section commander hadn't given the move order either.

The platoon commander gave an order splintering the darkness. Neither Scout One got up nor dared the section commander lead the section. Fallen in bafflement, life, at the moment, unprecedentedly loved it.

'Oye, One Section! Don't you get up?' platoon commander snapped, 'On your feet and move.'

The fearless platoon commander got up at once. Immediately he directed the section commander, Corporal Ram, 'Move your section right now.'

At the taxing moment nobody was ready to sacrifice their lives. But the guts of the platoon commander, who was a man of huge and muscular body and having an experience of fighting against guerrilla in the Borneo war in the late 1960s, made the whole section brave and energetic. We moved towards the directed destination in search of enemies.

Nothing could be seen except the darkness. Nothing could be heard except the wheeze of wind. Nonetheless, we kept moving forward tactically in the mission to find out the enemies. We didn't know whether enemies would find us first or vice versa.

In course of the task to the given destination, our eyes fell on a shape that looked like a shed or a hut, on which enemies stir was said to be taking place. We observed the hut seen at the skyline at a considerable distance through the night vision we had. we also used the Individual Weapon Sight for clearer view. Going further ahead, we tried to steal a peep of the enemies.

Nothing we saw. Nothing we heard. We heedfully moved ahead and besieged the shed-like house. Nothing was found inside the zinc roofed and plank covered ruined house. We didn't find any trace of enemy's presence. The mission assigned to us now was accomplished.

Now, we had to return to the pick up point to board the Land Rover and return to the defensive location. We took the same route back as we had gone to search the enemies. The possibility of encountering the enemies was highly likely while going forward rather than coming back, So, there was obviously less fear for us on returning.

'Enemy! Take cover.'

As soon as we heard the order from the front, we went to prone position on the ground and took firing position. Once again, my heartbeat abnormally increased. I thought the confusion was the reason that put us in a state of dilemma than fright. If enemy appeared he would instantly be killed. Dilemma prevails if enemy is not visible in the darkness. Suspicion makes the heart leap up: Where is the enemy hiding? Is he trying to fire at me?

Possibility of blue on blue or friendly forces shooting at friendly forces especially at night, could also happen. Merely a few days back, we had heard a very bad news that there was firing taken place between our friendly forces in course of night patrolling.

I assumed we encountered the enemies while searching them. For a long time, we tried to pin point the movement but we could hear nothing. After observing through the night vision, it looked like a human crawling ahead. We were certain about it. Now, we ought to finish the enemy in an ambush. We were ready to shoot the enemy. We were all agog to open the fire and breathlessly waited for the enemy's arrival.

No, enemy didn't come at all. Observation through the night vision went on. The supposed enemy approached nearer and nearer so we figured them out- what a deceive ! it was not a throng of Argentine enemies but it turned out to be a flock of sheep. It was so difficult to exactly recognise the enemy in the darkness. Life is ever at high risk in the war no matter how much we attempt to be fearless. Human life is never free of fear but fear germinates from within.

In the darkness of the night, the wind blow also sounds like human speech. Any constant object in the feeble moonlight also looks like an enemy approaching towards us. Perhaps it is all because of tension and psychological alarm.

We returned to the same location, where the platoon commander with Land Rover and its driver were waiting for us. We boarded the Land Rover after our reunion and headed back. It may have been our luck that we all returned safely having completed the mission. It was well past midnight as we got back to our trenches. It was drizzling and windy too. And the cold condition was further escalated by wind blowing.

We took rest in rotational basis and carried out night duty too. As I woke up at dawn to be readied for stand to, I found myself soaked in rainfall so did my trench mate, Gunner Purna Bahadur. The sleep deprived as well exhausted body gradually turned out to be freshen up as I got wet in cold water. We became more and more alert as the day progressed.

Chapter 6: Confronting the enemy

Tuesday June 8 1982

Conditions, which had been bad to start with, actually got worse. The weather was freezing, and even the boiled tea in mess tin would get cold within minutes. Arctic clothing meant to protect us from freezing conditions was also not warm enough. We had Goretex suits that were waterproof and would be warm enough, but we were not allowed to wear them as the suit would rob against the thigh and would generate cracklings during movements. The rubbing sounds would easily give away our presence to the enemy and would pose danger.

The section commander, Corporal Ram, came back from platoon O Group. In his trench, I called all the members of the section for order from the section commander. Corporal Ram issued an order to us. According to Corporal Ram, we would have to leave the defensive location where we had stayed for a week and now ought to move to Bluff Cove together with A and D companies.

The trenches we had dug down were like our houses to give us safety and security. But when we were ordered to leave them, we had to do so.

We had received the order to go to Bluff Cove by ship. So, we moved forward heading towards the jetty that was constructed on the lake like seashore close to Goose Green Settlement. The jetty was built with wooden planks over the concrete pillars which was considerably long just like a bridge. We each had heavy bergen on our backs that was slowing down our normal pace. Due to single file formation, half of the company was walking over the jetty to board the ship and the other half was still walking on the ground. While we were walking in a row over the wooden planks in the afternoon, there flew a couple of enemy aircrafts right over us heading east. The sound was defining and terrifying.

'Enemy aircraft! Stand to!' our platoon commander roared.

The order was issued. I deduced an apocalypse in life was going to take place. We were ordered not to board the ship we were about to board. Hurriedly, in a huffing and puffing motion, we dispersed over the jetty and returned to the fringe of the settlement. What will happen now? Will the Mirages return again? Dilemma dwelled upon our hearts. All of us would turn into ashes on the spot provided the fighters made a ground assault while we were walking over the jetty. Luckily, the situation developed differently.

As per the order, we got ready to counter the enemy's aerial attack. We took firing positions leaning against the iron pillar, hillocks, corner of the house; wall or whatever support was available to protect us from enemy fire. Meanwhile, we heard unproven news that the enemies were going to land through the parachute. While awaiting the enemy's arrival by pointing the rifle towards the firmament I devised a plan: the enemy can't fire aiming at me while descending down the parachute. So, I will very comfortably kill them one after another.

While getting ready to fire the rifles and machine guns at the enemies just like me, I thought, everybody of my comrades were focusing only killing the enemies and nothing else. Gunner Purna Bahadur was also ready to fire at the enemies by loading almost a meter-long ammunition belt of machine gun.

We waited for the enemies approximately two hours. Neither they made aerial assault nor did they parachute to launch ground attack against us. Eventually, the battalion plan to go to Bluff Cove was cancelled. Instead, we received the order to return to the trenches we left behind. By the time we rejoined the trenches it was already getting dark. I felt as if I had returned to a very safe place with no fear. Our company didn't have to bear any loss of life as we didn't come under enemy attack yet.

Late at night, we heard painful news that came through the radio set. It could be the same enemy fighters, that flew eastbound over us while we were about to board the ship, had bombarded over a British warship named Sir Galahad, killing many of our fellow co-warriors of the First Battalion, Welsh Guards. They were also part of Five Infantry Brigade and had sailed together with us from Southampton to South Georgia. This was a devastating news for us as there had been fifty precious soldiers' lives perished in a single spot. We deeply sadden by this news as we had been on the same mission and fighting the enemy shoulder to shoulder. This news stunned us. It had a profound impact over us all. Our rising morale was promptly sunk. Does war mean ruin of life that dies sooner or later?

While the Welsh Guards were planning to get to Bluff Cove from Fitzroy and about to reach their destination, suddenly, there had been Argentine Sky Hawk Fighters attack over Sir Galahad. The ship had been hit by missiles fired from enemy aircrafts that destroyed Sir Galahad, killed and injured soldiers.

The moment we were mourning for the grave memory of the deceased, perhaps Argentina was celebrating the carnage. Argentina would probably have also thought that success was certain for them. The Junta ruler must have been clapping the moment Sir Galahad was turning into ashes. (After the turmoil of war was over, we were stupefied to watch the video of the Argentine aerial attack over Sir Galahad and the grave loss Welsh Guard had to bear. The bombarded ship was covered with fire flame and smoke. The scene was capable enough to tear the heart of any lion-hearted into pieces. As the bodies were bursting into ammunition and fire, soldiers were jumping into the freezing water of the sea for the sake of protecting their lives. None of us watching the heart-wrenching video could stop ourselves from crying.

Wednesday June 9 1982

Due to the heavy loss caused by the enemies' unexpected assault, our battalion's plan of going to Bluff Cove was postponed. We stayed in the trenches almost throughout the whole day in order to face the enemies' possible attack. Section commanders were called at platoon command post as soon as company commanders were reported to have gone to battalion order. Though the situation changed and confusion arose, we were in ready position assuming that at any moment we might get an order to move ahead.

Our section commander came back from platoon command post receiving an order that the following day we again had to move towards Bluff Cove. What is the reason behind this compulsory move to Bluff Cove after so many soldiers were killed? This question was suppressed inside me somewhere down in the bottom of my heart. We had difficulty understanding the reasons behind us moving to Bluff Cove. I thought possibly, Bluff Cove was the gate way to the war, or departing point, from where the real war would start.

The strategy got change, as did the means of transportation. This time, we had to fly into the enemy area by helicopters instead of sailing in a ship. Making necessary preparation for next day, we got time to clean our rifles and machine guns in rotation. The damp weather was causing the weapons to get rusty easily. We cleaned and oiled the weapons so that it could fire rounds without any stoppages to kill the enemy. We dusted, cleaned and dried rounds. Magazines and grenades that were kept in the pouches were checked and so did the machine guns' spare belts. While I was doing all these, I kept thinking of killing enemy to sustain my own life. Life became even dearer and more loveable. On top of the love to life, the love even grew more for rifles and bullets. I thought that was the only way I would be protected. Loving the rifles and ammunitions ultimately meant to me a love for life.

Thursday June 10 1982

We were in helicopters following low and hidden surfaces in order to avoid the enemies' eyes. During this tactical flights towards Bluff Cove, helicopters were flying just over a few metres off the ground as if it was going to strike the land. As the news was pervasive that the enemies were shooting the helicopters down by anti-aircraft weapons. Therefore, there was no other option available for the pilot other than staying low to safely transport the troops. Avoiding the foes' eyes, the helicopters dropped us off about twenty one miles west from Stanley, the capital of Falkland Islands. As we landed, we saw Artillery guns mounted in the area for supporting fire. All the Artillery guns were camouflaged so, the enemy would not see its presence in the open grassy field. However, guns barrels were exposed and might give away enemy a clue.

The geo-structure of the area was adverse, particularly unsuitable for ground forces. There were no trees. No bushes. No holes or pits. Nothing was available to obscure us from enemy's sight. On the open grassy land enemies could easily detect us from miles away. Being the professional troops of the British Army, we had the capacity to transform uneasy to easy, adverse to supportive and unattainable to attainable. We proceeded ahead utilising the skills and tactics that was suitable according to the ground structure. The low ground that we had been advancing towards Stanley was flat and open and surrounded by a range of medium height rocky hills on our both sides. Theses medium high hill ridge could serve a very strong foundation for security thereby supporting us to be an eventual winner of this ongoing war.

We were advancing in an arrowhead formation which was believed to be the most suitable formation in open ground. We, One Section, were the leading section of the leading platoon. Meaning we were sharp head of the arrow. Being the first target of the enemy. Stanley, believed to be the enemies' stronghold, had not been expected to reached without a big fight. We heard sounds in the sky never heard before. The sizzling sounds, over us high in the sky suddenly burst out right behind us. Immediately after the bomb blasted, we heard a faint voice ordering us, 'Take cover.'

We instantly got low on the ground then crawled to get to the covers to protect ourselves from enemy bombarding. The Argentine artillery and mortar bombs blasted out of the blue as if it to welcome us to the battleground. Some of us ran towards rocky slopes in order to get to a stronger protection that would not be destroyed by enemy bombardments. We, One Section took cover whatever firm objects were available around us on the ground. I and Gunner Purna Bahadur shared the same cover of a big rock. Obviously the machine gunner and the gun controller were needed to be together to put up an effective firepower. Covering behind the big rock, we readied ourselves to face the enemy.

The enemy fired their cannons that exploded over us. The alarming screeches stopped. All of us turned into like deaf and dumb. I heard nothing at all other than bombardment and bombs blasting around the area where we had been taking cover. Firing ceased once again. So terrible was the momentary firing! How would it be if the firing continues?

'Take the injured in the cover.'

Somebody came forward for rescue.

'Platoon Sergeant! Where is the first aid bag?' Someone was administering treatment to the soldier got hit by enemy bombardment.

During the rescue work of the wounded, the dispersed soldiers gathered in their own sections and platoons. In the uncontrolled vertiginous situation, I felt a tinge of terror on the face and the black shadow of death was whirling around our heads. I thought, soldiers' lives on the battleground might burst in a single firing.

Gurujis would tell us in the training, 'A bullet doesn't have eyes so it might hit anyone.'

I concluded the statement was true when the news came that our B Company 2IC (Second in command) Captain (QGO) Dal Bahadur Sunuwar sustained injuries in the firing. He was not the only one who got injured from B Company, Riflemen Jit Bahadur Limbu and Bali Prasad Rai got wounded, too.

We were also told that there had been sustained a serious injury to Lance Corporal Gyanendra Rai, being hit on his abdomen. The news of co-warriors' injury embittered my heart. Anything undesirable might happen in the war.

A helicopter rescuing the wounded took them towards the ship named SS Uganda, a neutral hospital ship declared under the Geneva Convention, which was sailing against the vigorously powerful waves of the Atlantic Ocean. Putting the cross in red colour on the white background, the SS Uganda was transformed into a hospital during the war which had taken a responsibility of treatment of the wounded from the both sides without discrimination.

Our company was reformed taking the advantage of the moment when enemies' firing and bomb explosion momentarily stopped. Devoid of the heat and fervour of the sun, the day looked as if it was defeated and shivering with the cold.

The enemy's artillery firing had just stopped in the evening because they might not detect our figure anymore in the darkness.

Our 105 artillery guns that were mounted for operation were close by us. The enemy's mortar and artillery again simply began to burst as though it had forgotten to burst. It didn't burst continuously but intermittently. We had taken position in very good coverage, so its impact was not as harsh as it was in the day. Because of the dampness of the land, the impact of the bomb explosion was less effective. Had the land been hard, the death toll would have certainly risen.

As the night came about, the reminiscence of family tormented me. While the bombs were blasting I gravely remembered my father who had been entrapped in the Japanese assault in the Burmese jungle. He used to relate the story of his fight in Burma and safe return home. We would eagerly listen to the whole exciting narrative. I did reminisce my sister and brothers too. I also deeply remembered my phupu, (the younger sister of my father) who would love me a lot in my childhood.

In the extremely cold night I imagined many things about my would be life partner whom I had neither seen nor met. My deep love to her was in my heart, as if it was germinated in the fertile nursery deep down in my heart. How bizarre the phenomenon called love is! It makes us submissive and depressed. However, I tried to control myself. I offered a bhakal, (a sacred and sometimes secret promise to deities to offer something if wish is fulfilled) to God. I wished I could fulfil my duty defeating the enemy. Overwhelmed with feeling, perhaps I was pleading to me to grant my life.

In the tranquil night, after a while, artillery did burst afar. Perhaps, the enemy fired it in order to give a notice of its continuous presence in the area. Or it might have been fired by our troops to exasperate the enemy. Except this, we didn't hear any other firings and bomb blasts throughout the night

Friday June 11 1982

After digging shell trenches, we performed sentry duty in rotation and slept in the sleeping bag covering with poncho. In the morning, we found ourselves enveloped in the snow. The grassy land and hills around us were contracted by the light snowfall at night.

The artillery guns nearby, only exposing barrel outside, were covered inside camouflage net. While performing duty at Stand To, nobody and nothing was present on the desolate field. There was not any commotion except our friendly force under the area-clearing-patrol mission set out to the slope in expectation of running upon enemies. After the confirmation of enemies' absence in the specified area, the friendly force returned safely to its location.

The whole day long we busied ourselves to prepare further tasks protecting artillery guns at their own place. The section commander informed us the British troop was moving ahead making an assault over enemies by besieging Stanley from all directions. From the very beginning of the war we were told enemies were holding strong defence in the Stanley area. Hence, we anticipated the ultimate and implacable war would take place in Stanley.

After a couple of days of the commencement of war, British B 52 Stealth Bomber had destroyed the only airfield located at Stanley expecting that Argentina could not use the air field for its comfort. However, for fighter jet to fly after a run, even a short runway would suffice so that the Mirage, which was made in France, was dispatched in the mission to attack us using the same runway. Furthermore, from the main land of Argentina, which was located at the distance of only 300 miles from the Falklands, the enemies could launch their missiles straight.

The British troops were advancing towards Stanley from three different directions. The enemies were besieged in Stanley as our troops obstructed their course even from the sea. The scope of their movement, motion and supplies contracted. Both British Aircraft carriers HMS Invincible and HMS Hermes had been in active service in Falklands from where, Sea King Harrier fighters successfully carried out their missions over enemy.

From the early morning till evening, the helicopter kept dropping under slung load packed in net nearby us. Among the dropped goods, artillery bombs were more and small arms ammunition in fewer amounts. Though we had enough ammunitions, additional ammunitions were supplied to us. We had got to move ahead towards Stanley following the policy of 'destroying and securing the enemy location.' For this mission, the section commander, Corporal Ram issued a warning order to us for the task of launching an attack over Mount Tumbledown and Mount William respectively. We prepared for oncoming battle and waited for move order.

The Argentine artillery attack, which had bombarded the day before, both at day and night over us which caused loss as well as disappointment, dwindled. The reason of its silence was revealed to us afterwards. Our reconnaissance helicopter identified the location of enemy artillery and destroyed it by launching missiles. This news raised our morale enough.

From the point of commencement of the war Rifleman Uttarman was frowning every time. There was not an exception of it at this moment of war. His wrinkled brow revealed he was terrified. I could conspicuously read the whole narrative of his life on those wrinkles. However, the news of destruction of enemies' artillery I guessed helped staggeringly flow a small canal of delight on the lines of his brow. His countenance looked somehow bright by assurance. Somehow it looked excited as well. This news brought him a little outside otherwise he would ever be leaning against a support. I realised fright is frightful.

The paleness worn on Corporal Ran Bahadur's face all the way from Church Crookham didn't decline yet. Even a fairly meagre moonlight didn't rise on Ran Bahadur's gloomy face. Most of the soldiers' face wouldn't wear the sunlight of delight but at least a little degree of brightness could be visible. However, it was mysterious why Corporal Ran Bahadur's face looked like the darkest night though he was in the Reserve Section. The meaning of the darkest night not changing into the moon-lit night was he shrivelled like a tobacco leaf by anxiety.

Evening approached and then night. Contrary to our expectation, the comparatively peaceful night, at once, changed the way weather changes. Those artillery guns within our security circle began to burst. The fatal rounds, fired out of the artillery gun barrels, began to fly in the sky creating hissing sound. Those rounds carrying death-message would fall and explode in the enemy's area.

The hair-raising artillery guns kept firing till late night shattering enemies' wish to live long. Taking the advantage of this situation, the warriors of the Second and the Third Battalion Parachute Regiment kept invading whole the night long at

Mount Longdon. Meanwhile, Marine Commando Force was also fighting an atypical war of the similar nature at Two Sisters Hill.

In the both nocturnal invasions, many enemies gave up the ghost. Willing to live full-fledged they were killed in early age. Hundreds of them were captured. This news made us more excited and determined on our journey to success.

Chapter 7: The attack on Mount Tumbledown

Saturday June 12 1982

For two days, we were fully prepared and readied to attack over the enemy positions, but we did not receive move order that we were waiting for.

In the early morning, just like very faint sun rays of delight were seen to have fallen on Rifleman Uttarman's face. However, Corporal Ran Bahadur's face was unchanged. Exactly alike was his gloomy face with the tasteless day of the overcast Falklands.

The morning scene of the prisoners of war being escorted and leading away was pitiable. They were captured during previous night's attack and were seen lengthy queue walking with no weapons. Who are the most unfortunate, soldier who are killed or the ones being made prisoners of war? Of course, most people would reply that being a POW is better than being dead, but all the same the question seemed reasonable to me. There arose a question within me. Wearing cheerless appearance, they were meekly following their own life as POWs like sheep and goats.

In the slightly brightened day, the helicopter began to drop the artillery's rounds again. We surmised rounds were being dropped to the ground for another assault at night. The meaning of dropping those rounds over yonder was - unnoticed death of so many lives.

We were hankering for rations as much as we were for rounds. The rations that had been issued to us had almost run out.

'Forty-seven guruji!' Scout Two, Rifleman Purna Prasad Limbu came closer to me and asked, 'How about ration supply, are we not getting any?'

'Let me ask the platoon Sergeant,' I replied.

I went to the platoon headquarters carrying my rifle in alert position. I returned with the assurance of rations supply that rations would be supplied either on the same day or the following day.

We did have the spare biscuits, tinned mutton, tinned pork and tinned beef with tea boiled in mess tin. Somehow, we managed our hunger.

'Hey, forty seven! Any spare hexamin?' Lance Corporal Ratan Bahadur asked me.

I gave him the hexamine (hexamine stove is a foldable and tiny cooking stove that uses hexamine fuel tablet which burns smokeless and can be carried in a pouch) that was with me.

I was cleaning the rifle. After a while, I heard Lance Corporal Ratan Bahadur speak, 'Hello forty-seven! Take this chocolate.'

I looked at him. He was standing straight holding the black rubber water bottle cover from which hot chocolate drink was vaporising. It was great of Ratan guruji. Machine gunner Purna Bahadur and I shared the chocolate. My body, though gone numb due to the cold, regained energy.

It was very important to us to save energy so we could launch an attack over Stanley. It was also equally important to have triumph in the war. If our physical strength weakened, it would directly affect the morale of the troops. Therefore, rations had to be distributed as soon as possible. Since assurance of rations supply was given, we curiously cast our military eyes upon every arrival of the helicopters with underslung loads.

As we all were waiting long enough for rations, we saw loads after load only contained artillery's rounds being supplied. Having been witnessed these loads, then we understood the necessity of weaponry and its management to defeat the enemy is the first priority in the war. Other admin supplies are of less importance.

The moment the loaded cartoons of composite rations were detectable from afar; all the warriors were thrilled. Under the supervision of the platoon Sergeant and section 2IC (second in command) of every section, rations got distributed. The varieties of tinned meat, biscuits and chocolate packets wouldn't adjust in the pouches that were full of ammunition. They were kept in bergens.

The Second Battalion, Scots Guard and First Battalion Welsh Guard moved ahead for Mount William in the evening. Our battalion, Seventh Gurkha Rifles remained in the same place since we didn't get move order. The sound of bomb blast was intermittently heard at night so that I guessed our co warriors perhaps, didn't need to fight a deadly war. Unlike the previous night the artillery guns located nearby us also didn't continuously fire. The ones who fired artillery guns perhaps took the strategy of firing and keeping quiet in a regular interval.

On one hand, fright of war, on the other hand an atmosphere of severe cold. As on the previous night, yet again, we remained awake more and fell asleep less. The poncho spread over the sleeping bag to avoid the cold would be damp by our own vapour. The following morning, the ground would turn whitish almost with snow, if not, with the frost.

Sunday June 13 1982

From the early morning, we got ready to board the helicopter in order to attack the foes at night. Helicopters began to transport the artillery guns hanging towards the new firing location. The sight of the flying helicopters with artillery guns underslung would look so beautiful as if eagles were flying away carrying chickens.

Our turn to fly out came when artillery were transported. Leaving the heavy bergens packed with goods on its own place, we boarded the Sea King Helicopters carrying all ammunition, weapons and light goods necessary for assault.

The Sea King kept flying avoiding enemies' eyes and almost touching the ground. It landed us about two miles away from the enemies' defensive position. We got the evidence of the failure of our attempt to avoid the enemies' eyes only at the moment when the enemies' artillery shells began to land along with our landing. Bombs dropped all over the ground as we were getting off the helicopters. The only way to protect ourselves from the shells being dropped from miles away was to reach to the cover as soon as possible. Around thirty of us breathlessly ran uphill together to take cover behind a rocky hillock. The time was three o'clock in the afternoon. I heaved a sigh of relief after taking a cover. I was together with the Gunner on the right hand side of a little bit secured hill that was capable of avoiding enemies' eyes. I thanked God for my survival.

Suddenly, I saw a couple of Mirage fighters and another couple of Harrier fighters following them, right over us darted southward as if they were chasing each other. A British soldier, who was positioned in front of me fired a magazine full of ammunition in order to try to hit the fighter. It made no difference; the fighter kept on flying.

Once we positioned ourselves in a firm cover, a reconnaissance patrol for final assault over Mount Tumbledown dispatched. The patrol was comprised of company commander, platoon commanders, detachment commanders that were attached to the company and a radio operator. The rest of us remained at the same location waiting for their return. During that time, we made final preparation for attack. The artillery of the enemies were still being fired in the similar fashion as it was fired the moment we got down the helicopters. British artillery also kept firing as did theirs. Two ways of bombarding was spoiling the earth as well as the firmament. The fright of death prevailed all around as though all optimism of life had collapsed.

Changing the dubious environment into more frightful a fighter jet directly above us took a hold for a moment in the firmament and dropped missiles.

'Oh my goodness! Death is sure to claim me today,' I gave up my hope of being alive by looking at the dropping bomb.

Unexpectedly the bomb changed its direction after falling around fifteen feet. The bomb disappeared flying in enemy direction in full speed. Unknown about the methodology of missile launch of Harrier Fighter, which was very effective for ground assault, I was astounded. Thank god! I survived despite my hopelessness.

After the return of company Reconnaissance Group, an order was issued at platoon and section level for night attack. Corporal Ram issued the order to us to attack Mount Tumbledown. According to the order, we, One Section yet again were given to take the role of leading section. Being as the 2IC, I had already allocated ammunition to every individual in my section. Pouches were full of spare bullet fed magazines, grenades and spare cartridges whereas bodies were girdled with the GPMG belts. Each section was issued two 66 MM anti-tank rocket launcher that also was hung on the side of shoulder. I felt as if war meant a huge congregation of weaponry.

Leading section was the first target of the enemy. Somehow, I was disheartened. I did not know why only our section always had to take the role of leading section to face the enemy's first firing. Everybody dearly loves their life. A volcano of resistance gravely grew inside me. I looked at the obliged section commander. His appearance wore gloom. Who could stand against the order? Military life is always governed by order and discipline so, we had no other options other than putting ourselves under the yoke of order.

Compelled to be at the front in the Mount Tumbledown attack, except Corporal Ram, we were immature bachelors who had not even been to home for six months first leave. Perhaps, this could have been the reason why we were always ordered to be at the front. Always obliged to take the leading role and becoming the first target of the enemy, Four Platoon One Section was comprised of myself 21163247 Rifleman Ganesh Kumar Rai (Gun controller and section 2IC), 21163854 Rifleman Purna Bahadur Rai (GPMG gunner), 21163883 Rifleman Dipak Tamang (GPMG gunner), 21164255 Rifleman Amritman Rai (Scout One), 21164326 Rifleman Purna Prasad Limbu (Scout Two) and 21165159 Rifleman Uttarhang Limbu (Rifle one). H hour was Eleven o'clock at night, that was the exact time that the attack on Mount Tumbledown should get started. Waiting for the time to move ahead, we were anxious as well as terrified. We talked about our pains and pleasures among us.

'Why should only we always to be on the front line?' Machine gunner Purna Bahadur, who would normally not talk if not necessary, angrily complained to me.

His complaint was reasonable. We were always leading at the front line. As a section 2IC, I didn't have any answer worth giving. Section commander Corporal Ram had to make a complain to the platoon commander while receiving order. Perhaps he didn't complain.

'The section commander had to complain the platoon commander. What can I do if he doesn't do so?' I explained the reality.

'It's quite unfair. Why should we always be at the front line?' Dipak, another machine gunner said. 'Are our bodies made up of iron?'

All of us expressed our fretfulness buzzing with the complaint that all soldiers should walk in a single extended line. The countenance of Corporal Ram, who was keeping quiet after issuing an order to us, was as gloomy as the weather of the Falklands. Possibly, Corporal Ram was thinking of his wife and children back in Nepal.

Meanwhile, the platoon Sergeant, Sergeant Agendra Bahadur Limbu distributed additional field dressings that were applied on the injuries caused by firing in order to control bleeding. The distribution of additional field dressing was a tocsin of the fearsome war. The fear impending death was looming around.

We got disheartened for we had to make an assault on the spot where the enemy was supposed to be strong. My confidence that I would survive simply vanished.

My psyche was tormented with the questions like how I would die, on which part of my body the bullet would hit and how I would breathe my last gasp. I wished to die by a single bullet at once if death would take my life in the battlefield. If I got critically wounded or disabled, my family would have to take the burden of looking after me. My situation was considerably different from others. I was bachelor and I didn't have mother. Presumably, my tension was not much grave. However, nobody is ready to die no matter how much lonely they are. The network of worldly love, affection and attachment makes one think seriously, at least once, prior to death in the war no matter how much lion-hearted they seem to be.

I found my own heart so heavy and difficult to control as though the load of thousand kilograms of iron was constantly pressing it.

As soon as darkness fell over the Falklands, we stepped ahead to face the enemy and attack at Tumbledown. The footsteps pressed with heavy heart wouldn't be light anymore. Anything is possible to happen in war: death, survival or injury. Definitely, there would be no guarantee of warrior life in the war.

A sense of fear had germinated in my mind the moment I heard the news at the desolate landscape of Belize for the first time, that the war was staged at the Falklands. The latently sprouting fear, in course of time, grew into an excrescence of fright in my heart.

When we came to the battlefield, on one hand our proximity increased with enemies' bombs and firings, on the other hand, the volume of fright kept expanding. The moment the war became fatal and appeared in its hideous form, the fear of death reached to its culmination. We were hardly dragging our life carrying the wounded heart scratched by the cruel claws of the apprehensive war. I had never seen life so helplessly asking for the alms for its continuation.

Avoiding the enemy bombardment our footsteps stopped after reaching Assembly Area. Exactly at the fixed time, at eleven o'clock in the night, Second Battalion Scots Guard attacked at the Tumbledown Ridge. When artillery and mortar's bombard was added in the small arms such as Rifles and GPMGs firing, the ambience turned to be more terrible. While launching the supporting firing from the hills, the wriggles of the fire-like burning tracer round (a special kind of round which is used in order to indicate the target i.e. enemy position) would look scarifying. The tracer rounds fired from the both sides would strike against one another and resultantly some of them flew towards the firmament and others fell to the ground. The scene would not only affright but allure as well. We were observing the terror of attack in its culmination while waiting in the gorge between two hills for our turn to attack the enemy on top of Mount Tumbledown. There were nonstop firings from both sides going on in the darkness.

During our training, we were taught not to use the tracer round at night as of course it would reveal our position. But why was the tracer round used in such moment in the pitch darkness? My tender brain fell into the maze of question. Those involved in covering fire were instantly targeted. As a result, after the artillery and mortar bombard, they turned to be silent. Their loss was considerable and terrible for both sides.

The splintering and whistling sound of the bombardment were accompanied by a shriek- 'Ouch mom!'

The artillery and mortar bombs exploding on the hill top suddenly fell in the Assembly Area, where we were still waiting to move forward. Terror reigned. We were unknown whether it missed the track or firing was made after identifying a new target. There was no time to analyse it in a hurry of saving one's life.

The phenomena such as firing of artillery bombs everywhere, death of soldiers or sustaining injuries became too common. Coincidentally, an artillery shell falling on the ground and exploding and an unknown object hitting on my back occurred simultaneously. I nearly felt unconscious thinking that artillery bomb's shrapnel did strike me. I got flustered. I gave up my hope for life thinking that I was destined to die on the unknown land. All my colleagues dispersed in the darkness. They began to crawl or run.

Where could we go running away from the battle field? Everywhere there were enemies and fright. Where could we hide our fear in the battlefield that was strangled by trepidation? I hardly could move to another place to hide myself. In doing so my speed was not as slow as an injured person. I didn't feel any pain on my body, either. I guessed the object to strike terribly on my back was not a shrapnel of artillery bomb but could be a ball of soil drifted at the moment of bomb blast. How would I be able to reach to a secured place provided a bomb dropped on me?

At that moment, the shriek of the wounded mingled on the battlefield which was terrified by the artillery and mortar's roar, I thought humanity was defeated with cruelty. The entire ambience was growing nauseating with the heightening cruelty.

'Comrades! Don't leave me alone.'

After a moment's silence the same heart-breaking shriek.

'Do save me! I am not dead, yet.'

'Oh mother! I'm dying!'

Though the wounded were shouting for being afflicted by pain, the process of tearing the top of the hill with the bombard didn't stop. We heard the roaring sound of A Company 2IC Captain (QGO) Narain Prasad Rai in the form of authoritative order penetrating the shriek, request of the wounded, destructive sound of artillery bombard and the darkness, 'Hey soldiers! Don't run away. Get here to treat the wounded.'

The same voice was issuing an order once more, 'platoon Sergeant! Where is the first aid pack? Bring it over here at once.'

Stretchers were brought in, so that each reserve sections were having them in order to use exactly in such critical situation. They proved to be so useful. Doctors and medical staffs of Regimental Aid Post (RAP) without taking any care of their own lives, immediately got involved in treatment and rescue of the wounded. While the treatment was going on in the dim light, the agony and shriek of the wounded turned to be much more audible than the artillery' roaring.

We came to know that among the wounded, 21159185 Corporal Gyan Bahadur Rai's condition was critical after he sustained injury on his abdomen by a bomb's fragments. I couldn't imagine what kind of dream his wife or his family living in Nepal, saw the moment he was fighting a war against death in the battlefield whereas his entrails had come out of his body. Queries haunted me either she stumbled on the path or a crow casting a bad omen on the roof of the house. Or a haleso (a kind of bird as big as a pigeon having green neck, blue head and brown wings) mournfully cried on the branch of a tree or what kind of psychological condition she reached in after hearing about her husband's plight.

Despite the fact that the time was night, without caring the darkness, there came the helicopter and the wounded were timely rescued. The helicopter securely shifted the wounded in SS Uganda Ship, in which, for their additional treatment, medical staffs worked. What a controversial rule of war! Some people want to kill and others like to protect. Is life gifted to be killed or to live? I realised life outright stands in favour of life ignoring death even amidst dilemma.

On one hand, a deadly war was on going on the top of Mount Tumbledown, on the other hand, in the gorge below the continuity of falling of the artillery shells didn't break.

After the pestilent battle, finally, we heard the news that the Second Battalion, Scots Guard had defeated the enemies. After this victory, it was our turn to attack so we, A, B, and D companies moved ahead to reach to the start line (the pre-fixed place from where the attack begins). We had rightly guessed an easy victory wouldn't be possible in an uneasy war. On the rocky steeps, snowfall and darkness obstructed our journey. However, the silver like glittering snow in the little light of the moon made our trip somehow easy.

The moonlit night at two o'clock after the midnight was chilling. But we didn't feel much cold as we had to move ahead carrying ammunitions in addition to the belt of browning gun's bullet. At that time artillery and mortar's roaring had stopped except the intermittent firing. We hardly reached the start line avoiding the bombardment. In other words, we were fully ready to involve in the war.

We hurried off through the rocky path to reach Mount Tumbledown, that part of the mountain was recently captured by the Scots Guard.

It was the moment, we came across the reality that so many aspects affected the strategy and time in course of war. As per the war order, we should have defeated the enemies till then. Our plan was not materialised due to the adverse condition we had to endure.

Our company commander, Captain Lester Holy, issued the order to us to stay separately as he saw the soldiers huddled together in various groups at the time of bombarding and at the moment of stoppages. His order was absolutely right according to war strategy. Nobody wished more soldiers to die by a single firing. We were aware of the strategy however, we got huddled together just to keep the fright down. During the war period, we did feel that we would feel some consolation as intensity of fear would divide in group. Never was our wish to die in group. Nobody would like to die in the alien land. We were not its exception either.

With the supporting firings of artillery and mortars throughout the night, the onslaught continued to attack the enemy's positions along the hills and besiege Stanley. Perhaps, enemies were exhausted by the bombardments targeted not only from the land but also from the warships sailing on the ocean. Following the 'advance, destroy and clear strategy' the British troops continuously moved ahead launching attacks on Argentine Defensive positions.

The meal we had taken the previous evening was still sustaining us. Even if we were starved, this was not the right time to get fed rather it was the pinnacle of time to attack the enemy. Which was our priority.

As it was our turn to attack the foes climbing up the top of the Mount Tumbledown, the whole night long, we busied ourselves on the same mission. The enemies' artillery bombs were rapidly blasting and falling on the rocky top of Mount Tumbledown. Those explosions were obviously obstructing our movement so, we were not gaining our expected speed. The vibration of the serially exploded bombs on the top of the north faced cave, from where Tumbledown top could be reached, the cave kept quaking. Furthermore, our hearts shuddered along with the cave. At the frightening moment, fortunately we didn't have to lose anything on our side since the rocky cave served as a strong armour to protect us from enemy's nonstop shelling. As we were expecting and waiting for an appropriate moment to move ahead, the time of daybreak got near at hand.

Chapter 8: The raging war

Monday June 14 1982

The intensity of artillery and mortar bombards increased instead of decreasing. Possibly, the enemies once more had got supplied of more bombs and ammunition. The Argentine bombs fell like hailstones. As the grassland was desolate the loss of life and property was zero. However, our military psyche grew spiritless. Most probably, such a tremendous bombard was made according to the enemies' strategy to become triumphant in the war by discouraging our morale and getting us to surrender. Though the incessant bombard terrified us, it couldn't fragment our high morale.

Along with the artillery and mortar's vibrations, out of the blue, we heard and saw a weird type of firing sound and scene. After a bomb fell on the ground, that covered the circumference of five to seven meters, fire would abruptly burn for a moment and abruptly die out, and then white smoke spread around. This process made me surprise as it did the same to others. The land, in front of us, began to get fully covered by the white smoke as though heavy fog expanded over. In spite of the fact, that the lines of surprise spread over our face though, we didn't forget to wear respirators to protect ourselves from the poisonous gas.

Luckily, nature helped us, too. As the adage goes 'the dust to be swept is blown away by wind' the north bound wind blowing from the south pushed the poisonous phosphorus gas towards the horizon and it vanished. The gas firing continued for some time more.

Along with the end of the phosphorus gas attack, the battle-field suddenly turned to be pin-drop silent as though all the bombs to fire were run out. The unbelievably silent atmosphere was full of surprise. Why those all bombs and bullets firing till a moment ago shuddering the whole earth and the firmament, stopped suddenly? Wasn't there any fatal trick of enemies against us?

With the doubtful mind for a long time we stayed in the same position. We kept our ears acute and turned the eyes around. We didn't hear any firing anywhere. Neither the enemies showed up. We moved ahead as we had to accomplish the mission.

As soon as we got the news that A Company's fire support took the position, our strategy to move ahead became more certain and comfortable. The Fire Support Team had GPMGs in light role and sustain fire role ready to fire at the enemy. There was Mortar Section too, readied at Goat Ridge to provide covering fire to drop mortar's shells during our attack over the enemy.

We began to climb the steep hill in full alert. There was enemy's sniper firing coming from a distance from somewhere in front. Avoiding being hit from the sniper fire, we kept moving ahead. On the way, as we were about to reach to the top of the hill, we found a soldier, lying prostrate on the ground by the opponent's bullet. After a while, it revealed that the dead soldier was a Forward Observation Officer (FOO), a British Captain, perhaps he was on the hill to observe if the artillery bombs were falling on the right location. Unfortunately, he became the victim of the enemy's sniper.

Beside him, an upside-down rifle, half way down the barrel, was buried and a helmet was put on the rifle's butt. The poor soldier was killed while fighting. Such pitiable deaths seen only on cinema's screen were increasing as we moved ahead.

The top of Mount Tumbledown was just like a bull's hump, where we found blood oozing out of a fresh corpse of a British soldier. This soldier had just been killed by a bullet striking on his chest and oozing blood had turned white snow into red. The sight was so indigestible and choking. However, no alternative was left to us except carefully moving ahead avoiding sniper's eyes to eschew the possible death. We continuously moved ahead to run against the enemies.

After reaching the hill top, more consciously we got ready in the extended line to attack on enemies' position. Orders had already been issued in the previous evening, our B Company's main mission was to attack Mount Tumbledown, whereas D Company was ordered to attack Mount William.

While awaiting at the start line to launch an attack, the artillery and mortars' bombard was appalling the Argentine soldiers who were defending the hill top. After the bombs stopped, Machine Guns' roar was also more frightening to them. While making a counter attack against the enemy over Tumbledown, amidst firing around, my heart was filled with invincible courage rather than fright.

The British troops had been defeating the enemies from all around to besiege Stanley. As our section was the leading section, the possibility to be killed by the enemy bullet was much higher in comparison to the section in reserve. Despite the possibility, immensely trained about war strategy, we continued our mission being hidden from enemy's sight. The moment while the shrubs on the hill were delaying our advance, no less challenging it was to protect ourselves from the ambushes secretly set by the enemies and attack them. I didn't think anything except the enemies as I was wholeheartedly concentrated on them and determined to kill them as soon as they attempted to kill me.

Machine-gunner Purna Bahadur, too, carrying the GPMG in firing position, was moving ahead observantly almost in my own level to smite the swarm of enemies. On my right-hand side, Corporal Ram was in the middle of the section whereas a little farther, there were the co-warriors of Two Section under command of the section commander, Corporal Bhim Bahadur Limbu advancing in the same line.

On the distant top of the hill a throng of foes unexpectedly showed up. But the throng was not at the distance of small arms' range. We stopped taking a cover to protect ourselves. The throng dispersed the moment artillery and mortars' shells began to fall upon their heads. Many of them most have lost their lives and the survived ones could have hardly got protected themselves.

While advancing ahead by clearing Tumbledown, we found so many pits on the land caused by the artillery's strike. Also, we found empty trenches and bunkers that were left by enemies. The fresh corpses recently killed by artillery bombs were lying everywhere on the ground. In the trenches and around the bunkers, helmets, magazines with full of rounds, grenades and loose rounds were scattered everywhere.

It's never a valiant job to open fire and kill the enemies who are running away from the battlefield. It's not a symbol of bravery to kill the ones who have surrendered by raising both hands. If done so, it is a crime against the international norms of war. Furthermore, it is a cruelty against humanity. We disciplined Gurkhas didn't show demonic or criminal character committing war crime at all.

The moment we were clearing trenches and bunkers, we found some corpses there. We always treated enemies humanly no matter dead or alive. Soldiers are not made of iron, just like other men they are human too.

We cautiously and patiently put our fingers on the triggers and being alert to the utmost moved ahead to reach our destination.

We doubtfully thought whether the enemies were trying to make a surprise attack on us. If not, strongly located in the defensive position, they wouldn't run away leaving the bunkers and the trenches empty. Even in the silent moment such as this, when firing was not going on, our warriors' life was entangled amid questions.

'Grenade!' somebody suddenly shouted. In no time, we laid down the take cover position in order to avoid the fragments of a grenade explosion. But the grenade did not explode as our expectation. In course of moving ahead, one of our co-warriors happened to tread on the unexploded grenade that was left by enemy. Because of its danger of getting exploded he had warned us not to go around it.

On the move, through the hilltop, we saw our fellow warriors, on the right-hand side covering and clearing the low plain land, were moving ahead, like us, looking for the enemies. A little psychological relief we felt after seeing them. The battlefield situation developed in such a way as though the enemies didn't have any chance for victory.

Sapper Hill appeared in front of us in course of our advancement to the given mission. Down the hill, some miles away,

Stanley looked as if it sustained critical injuries in the war. Towards the smoke wriggles-rising Stanley many groups of the enemies were getting down. Presumably, they were moving towards the capital to get reorganised and put a decent fight against us, that was what we assumed.

Along with the rocky hill, there was cold wind tenaciously blowing, other parallel hills were also facing towards Stanley. Adverse weather had created difficulty. Moreover, the fall of small-sized hailstones was simultaneously affecting our movement and sight.

'Enemy! Enemy in the precipice!'

'Take cover!'

We had already taken the position before the order came. We would surely wait for the order if it was training. In a real war nobody needs to issue an order, that was what just proved to be reality. The situation itself would teach what action should be taken. Leaning against the steep land I did cast my eyes on the right hand side cliff. I saw the enemies on uniform who were carrying rifles and moving hither and thither. They turned to be our entire target. Those rifles carrying five enemies who were hiding in the cliffs came towards us raising their hands up as a symbol of surrender. They perhaps didn't feel humiliation in defeat but rejoiced their lucky survival.

As per our direction they came to us. We disarmed the enemies who just had surrendered. We checked their bodies thoroughly and found a page of newspaper in the pocket of an enemy. Ironically, the page contained a news report including the photographs clicked from various angles of vision projecting Gurkha soldiers' counter-attack, over the enemies. Even though the news report was in Spanish we could easily understand of the photo that displayed Gurkhas and the resplendent kukri. In spite of the fact that we had learnt some Spanish during our stay in Belize, the knowledge we had was not good enough to understand the news report considerably. Surely, it was propaganda.

I surmised Gurkha soldiers' photographs were borrowed from British newspapers and magazines. Sometimes in the history, Gurkhas had won battles and even wars through using their famous knife the kukri. However, it's not anything more than a nice joke to expect Gurkhas can defeat enemies with the help of their curved knife on the eve of the twenty-first century. Presumably, Argentina took the British propaganda news about Gurkhas as a way to exaggerate things in their, that is the Argentinians' favour.

Anyway, we were not unknown about the exaggeration of Gurkhas' bravery. False rumours were spread about us before the commencement of the Falklands war. This news report along with the photographs was a strong proof.

The British basically had applied a kind of strategy to win the war by creating psychological fright on the part of enemies. For this, the bravery demonstrated by Gurkhas in various wars was exaggeratedly advertised in the worldwide scale. Photographs in different poses making attacks and counter attacks against enemies were published in newspapers as well as broadcast on television screen.

Argentina took this situation as a clue and spread out baseless accusations. It falsely projected Gurkhas' stereotypical image of inhuman beast that fought under the influence of drug, slaughtered the surrendered opponent soldiers with the kukri and collected their heads and got ready to kill their own co warriors.

Irrespective of the propaganda spread out against Gurkha soldiers by Argentina, we behaved to those five Argentine prisoners of war according to the rule approved by Geneva Convention. They kept trembling by cold and fear. Neither were we exception of it.

'Hey Ganesh! Take out your kukri and slaughter them.'

My eyes suddenly turned towards the cruel voice that was issuing command against the international law approved by Geneva Convention. The one who issued an order to slaughter the war-prisoners was none other than the same black short Corporal, who didn't move anywhere, throughout the war period from the Reserve section out of fear.

'Don't be cruel and ridiculous!' I shouted back at him. 'We don't kill those who surrender! All of us would turn into ashes with shame if we fired at soldiers who had surrendered to us. Is it fair to talk about slaughtering them? You can slaughter them not me.'

Though we were Riflemen, a junior soldier, we had understood the reality that one should not foolishly think unfair is fair in war. In spite of the seniority of the Corporal, we would be senseless soldiers if we followed his proud behest verbatim. We never committed such kind of mistake throughout the war period.

Hearing my harsh and instant response his face turned to be much gloomier than the Falklands weather. Shamelessly he said, 'Ganesh! You are lucky. Your leave had been cancelled and you came to the war. Now you are going to receive a war medal.'

Corporal Ran Bahadur Limbu had lamented saying 'I am a pensioner, so I don't want to join the war' but now he looked pretty delighted by the excitement of victory like a child gifted with sweets and dolls. His fully eclipsed face looked so resplendent as though the light of ten different suns cast at once.

The moment British troop was moving ahead defeating the enemies through the attacks from all direction; Argentine troops ran away towards Stanley being unable to fight the British troops. They were perhaps silently signalling their passivity towards war staying in some small groups.

'Even if not single soldier remains alive, I will be fighting in Malvinas,' this valiant expression was not of anyone else but of General Mario Menendez who became the commander of Argentine troops after the Falklands war began. The meaning of his statement of course was: 'I won't accept my defeat at any cost.'

Mostly commanders, during war, make such kind of bold roar intending to dishearten enemies and encourage their own troops. General Mario Menendez's exaggerated roar was an example of the same.

Unfortunately, not only one but he had thousands of soldiers with him but all of them were afflicted by defeatist mentality. His meaningless roaring command was melting like the snow from the top of Mount Tumbledown as the way that was gushing down to get to Stanley and down below.

In fact, war is not merely the battle of armaments and ammunition. It is the battle of discourse as well. Threat and aplomb play considerable role to raise the troops' morale and win over the foes. However, in the case of the Falklands war, the threat of General Mario Menendez crumbled while his warriors were running away from the battlefield being unable to counter the British troops' superiority.

Looking at the enemies moving towards the dense smoke coming out of Stanley, we still remained at strong defensive position. I guessed those withdrawn enemies would get reorganised reaching Stanley and launch a fatal counter attack on us or stay in even stronger defence around Stanley and war of another phase would start. Probably, again we need to fight another fierce battle to vanquish them. Many soldiers needed to lose their life again.

The troubled time, when firing had stopped, was tranquil and confusing, too. Neither Mirage nor Harrier was on flight cracking the sky. There were no helicopters transporting troops and explosives. An unimaginable silence prevailed around as if no war took place and nothing devastated though a great demolishment tore down the area.

Even though the terrible war, causing great human casualty, was fought till now, the situation looked as if there was no trace of anomaly. As if there was no war but a drama about war was staged on the great theatre of the Falklands and it has recently been exposed. Warriors are throughout the battlefield. Arms and ammunitions are with them. Enemies are all around though they are running away. The order is issued for firing. The war hasn't been over yet. But why such tranquility? Is it reunion with the foes? Or has humanity got a tiny space after a terrible bad luck? The moment destroying the tranquility powerful wind was blowing and the snow-capped hills and slopes were drenched with blood, perhaps at the same time, signatures were put on the treaty paper. Perhaps risk was being calculated over the piles of corpses. If not, why such a great dilemma?

The afternoon while we felt like searching ourselves amidst desolation and doldrums, we received an important radio order coming from the platoon commander through the section commander.

'Argentina has surely accepted its defeat. It has been waving white flag in Stanley. Fifteen thousand enemies surrendered from both the east and the west Falklands. And they are under controlled by the British troops. Formal talk is ongoing to end the war. Then after the treaty paper will be signed. Now onwards, nobody will fire.'

It was almost 1400 hours local time while the cease fire order received.

I found the order not to fire in the battlefield quite confusing and unreliable.

However, the unproven news of the possible ending of the war somehow opened a new horizon of life. We were also said to remain cautious until the war formally ended as we were still at the battlefield. Following the order, we remained cautious as we were dutifully cautious from the beginning.

We, B Company, kept waiting for another order at the same point where we were and remained in the same position how we were. On the right hand side of the slope, where Four Platoon stayed, there was a high precipice. Members of company headquarter made a move to the direction of the same precipice. We saw squads of our co warriors advancing towards Stanley through the desolate plain valley. Staying on the hillside, we kept looking at their movement heading towards Stanley. At this stage I was desperate and tempted to reach Stanley to witness how the things were there. The place was not so far away from us. In comparison to other wars, the loss of life and property of the local residents in this war was meagre but the graph of psychological loss was absolutely rising up.

Our great desire to reach Stanley and directly view its real situation with our naked eyes fell into eclipse the moment we were given an order to spend the whole night at the place where we were. We had to take shelter in the cliff to protect ourselves from the adverse weather. And we also had to take a tremendous trouble to protect ourselves from the ambushes the foes had set everywhere.

I heaved a sigh of relief after securely reaching cave in the cliff. In the cave we found enemies' composite ration, arms and ammunitions and other necessary supplies they stored. We fortunately got what we hadn't expected for. We could fill up our hungry stomach with enemies' foodstuff.

We got our bergens back though late. Luckily helicopter dared bring the bergens that were packed with necessary stuffs despite the extremely adverse weather.

For collection of war souvenirs, the warriors began to move hither and thither. Almost all busied themselves to discover enemies' boot, helmet, cap, clothes, and gloves and so on. I didn't find anything worth collecting. My stubborn thought was that I should compulsorily find something made me roam around. I saw a British soldier relentlessly pulling out a pair of an enemy's high combat boot. I also got tempted that he was pulling a new high combat boot that seemed brown in colour. But he could not take it out no matter how much energy he was discharging. My plan was to take it out and make it my possession if he gave his endeavour up.

The boot looked like pressed by a blanket. The British soldier removed the blanket. Oh, my goodness! The scene, I saw, made me scared and sentimental. The reality got exposed why the boot didn't come out though a heavy force was applied to pull it out. Surprisingly, the new high combat boot was worn by a corpse. He seemed to have died in course of his health treatment. The guy expressed his indignation of being unable to take the boot off the feet by a shocking expression. I felt sorry to see the Argentinian's death and immediately gave up my search expedition.

While we were in the cave having hot tea and coffee, an order was circulated that the prisoner of war were needed to be escorted off to Stanley. After the escorts being ready, POWs were led away down the hill to the capital, Stanley. And the escorts returned few hours later.

We took shelter in the cave in order to protect ourselves from the snowfall accompanied by cold wind. We got to spend the night in the cave as though it was our home.

The food eaten some time back was not going to support further. Some tins and biscuit packets were in the pouch. As we were preparing the same food; in the meantime, the ones dispatched for patrol for clearing the area, came back. They discovered abundant rations left by the enemies in the cave. We got delighted to enjoy a party by using the same ration.

I had expected much more things to find in the enemies' rations but contrary to it, nothing more than biscuits, sweet packets and small cans of meat items. I didn't find their rations better than ours; presumably we were not habituated to it. However, it could help us to spend the night.

Throughout the night the rumour spread out that formal announcement of the end of war was going to be made. There was also snowfall which continued throughout. The circumstance grew in such a way as though no symptoms of sorrow and delight rose for both the defeated and the winner. In the cold night, taking the sentry duty in rotation, we comfortably slept in the cave. No anxiety was there that we were to be killed by the enemies or we had to kill the enemies. Our sleep in the cave was the first fearless sleep after many nights.

While thrusting ourselves inside the sleeping bag in the cliff's fissure the reminiscence of home considerably haunted me. I didn't know if the news of the stoppage of war served my rural settlement. My relatives and family members would be very happy provided they heard the news that I was alive. I thought a lot now about my would-be life partner living in a distant and desolate village. She surely remained unknown about my involvement in war, ending of war and my condition of being fit and fine. I wished to write a letter to her at the soonest. I spent the whole night in the figments of imagination. I also imagined how joyous they would be after seeing me within their company. But how pity it was that my loved ones were thousands of miles away in a remote hamlet where there was no access to any communication. And letters would take months to reach and back.

Tuesday June 15 1982

The first morning after the conflict in the Falklands was over, the environment was still terrible. Neither the wind speed had stopped nor had the cold decreased. The untimely expired corpses of the enemies were scattered everywhere unclaimed. Though I didn't want to behold, somehow my eyesight fell upon the shrivelled corpses. The corpses lying on the ground made me sentimental. Life, ironically, makes us act what is not thought. If they were alive possibly we would have turned into corpses. The rule of war is to survive by killing the enemy. It is to make the enemies fall in your clever snare and declare yourself great.

Stanley, the capital town, was not that far away from the location where we had been. In a particular distance, Stanley seemed like as if it was lying still and motionless. Perhaps the local residents, after the war was over, thought their snatched sleep again returned to their eyes. After experiencing the terrible war Stanley might have been trying to wake up out of its ailing fresh wound. Everywhere covered in snow, the Tumbledown area was as cold as it was vexatious. I wished I could get released from the place as soon as possible.

Stanley turned to be the confluence of the both winner and the loser soldiers. From Tumbledown I thought we saw Royal Military Police (RMP) with the assistance of fellow soldiers would be busied in controlling and observing the crowd of thousands of subjugated Argentine troops who surrendered and were made prisoner of war (POW) the previous day. A huge pile of prisoners of war, weaponry and paraphernalia would have got heaped in front of the British soldiers. Public life was not returned to its normality though the war had ended. Constant bombardments might have had ruined the public lives and properties. The local roads might get pits and holes here and there everywhere due to the artillery and mortars shelling. Local public must have been happy and joyous seeing the British win and returned them their freedom. The dead silently reported the war's absolute dreadfulness. The only international airport at Stanley also was like a patient in critical condition.

How long should we stay at the place where humanity lying supine to the ground was scorning humanity? When will these corpses of Argentines be collected and funeral rites be honourably conducted following cultural norms? Or will they remain there unclaimed and ignored forever? I thought I was growing much more sentimental, not as a soldier but just like the one who is human rights activist. Hence, I tried to be practical.

While we were still in the cliff, a message had been passed around that ten soldiers of our Gurkha battalion were reported to be wounded in the Falklands war. However, fortunately - very fortunately indeed - no Gurkha soldier had been killed.

Wednesday June 16 1982

We handed our weapon in. We were now victorious soldiers. All our faces were glowing with the sense of victory.

Meanwhile, in the morning time gathering I excitedly said to Uttar Man, 'Guruji! Didn't I tell you British troops would win the battle?'

Always anxious about his small children and young wife, poor Uttar Man had gone to the battlefield to carry out his soldiering duty. Uttar Man was vivaciously happy as was Tanka Bahadur.

'Really Ganesh! yes, I believe on what you say.'

Uttar Man's door of heart opened. The moment mirthfully he smiled, it looked as if the golden rays of the sun spread out in the gloomy morning of the Falklands. His innocent smile that wore in his entire face was just like the life that was full of life and happiness.

An order was issued to us to return to Goose Green. On one hand, my heart was thrilled with joy that I was about to return to a familiar place where I had spent more than a week in defence. On the other hand, sadness enveloped me that I could not reach Stanley though I was very close to it. I became too eager to see the town with my own eyes, because I had seen fellow comrades of other regiments advancing towards Stanley soon after the war was over.

In the afternoon, we returned to Goose Green by helicopter. The satisfaction brought by the ending of the war was tinged on the local residents' lips. They expressed cordiality upon our return. They hugged us and joyously congratulated and thanked us.

In the evening, the local residents organised a small cocktail party in our honour at the Community Centre. The community centre was not large enough to accommodate all of us in one go therefore, we participated in the party taking turn. Extremely delighted amiable residents of Goose Green talked to us the narrative of Argentine troops' misbehaviour.

In course of the conversation, in our group of half a dozen of people, a local resident of around forty years old said, 'I was born British. I want to live as a Briton. The Argentinians pointing their rifles at us, and ordered us not to observe a curfew inside our home. We were captives inside our own home!' Blood seemed to drop from his red cheeks. His eyes were shining. Furthermore, he expressed gratitude to us for we granted freedom to the Falklands from Argentine grip.

Nepalese food for us was never available from the day after we left Church Crookham for war in the Falklands. Favourite food of ours was not available even in the QE II ship let alone in the battlefield. After we came back to Goose Green from Tumbledown, a couple of times we got to eat mutton curry and rice as local resident's bestowal. Before this, during the battle, we survived eating biscuits and tinned meats from composite ration packs.

We, soldiers were much obliged to the honour offered to us by great hearted residents of the small settlement. We expressed a very sincere gratitude to them for systematically feeding the whole battalion that consisted of around six-seven hundred troops.

Thursday June 17 1982

Even though the ending of the war was announced, for it was our duty to be cautious about enemy activities so, we remained watchful on possible enemies' counter attack. In the meantime, army doctor and his assistants examined our health condition. Mostly we were enquired and examined about the effect of snow and cold that we were suffered from. Furthermore, enquiries were made assuming the possibility that some warriors might turn to be sick losing mental balance i.e. post battle traumatic syndrome due to the ghastly war. But we were not much suffering from the problem of such nature.

Our appointments with the regimental doctors were fixed as per the roll number of the companies and the platoons. Doctor and his assistants minutely observed our fingers and toes if snow had affected them. They asked us to move our limbs, fingers and toes.

Corporal Ram narrated his problem to the doctor that both of his calves tingled and caused difficulty while walking.

Almost all of our cheeks and lips were cracked by the chilling cold. Although the wounds of lips and cheeks were not paining throughout the war period it began to pain after our return to Goose Green. Ointment was given to us for healing by applying the ointment to the wound.

Goose Green was compelled to live watching the ruins of war around it. I didn't know when the war-terror experienced by the local residents would omit from their psyche. Or would the hangover trouble them throughout their life? Worthless fighter jets, motor vehicles were lying supine everywhere and empty trenches without soldiers looked joyless.

It was extremely urgent to clear such debris as soon as we could the earliest since they were posing danger and causing mental anguish and spreading negativity. To get rid of such war time horror, we were sent to different places to clear them. We endeavoured to grant security guarantee to the local residents and normalise their day to day life.

A Company was to secure Darwin settlement that was located nearby Goose Green in order to support and raise the morale of the local residents there. Similarly, C Company and D Company were involved in the security of Port Stephens and Fox Bay in the western Falklands respectively. We, B Company received the task to safeguard North Arm settlement. Battalion headquarters remained at the same place in Goose Green.

Chapter 9: The defence of North Arm

Friday, June 18 1982

A small liner ship was ready to take us to North Arm from the same Jetty, where just ten days back, while on our way to Bluff Cove, we were almost got killed in Argentine aerial attack.

It was ten o'clock in the night when we boarded the liner. The voyage was terrible as the nonstop oceanic waves yet again made our life hellish. With raging waves battering the ship continuously for twelve hours against the oceanic waves, we reached North Arm settlement at ten o'clock in the morning on Saturday 19 June.

The small ship, that was built with the purpose of transporting sheep, made me sick though nothing had happened to me in QE II and Norland. I threw up bitter water so much so, it was as if my bile duct was going to explode.

When I got off the ship in the morning, I was exhausted. My plight was almost of a patient.

It was not only me becoming sea sick, some of my friends' plight was not better than that of mine either. However, we were to reach a new place and meet new people. Despite my sickness, there was still some energy left on me to be a little excited.

Containing around thirty to forty houses, North Arm was a coastal settlement just like Goose Green. The local residents immensely honoured us. They showed their affections to us. They appreciated us for winning the battle against Argentina.

I forgot my trouble of vomiting whole night long.

The local residents, as much as possible, provided us with the urgent goods we needed. They showed cordiality so much so that they vacated their houses in order to ensure our comfortable stay.

Six of us from One Section Four Platoon, got our bedroom in Garden Section (a shed for keeping flower vessels). Our section commander Corporal Ram got handicapped and slept inside the sleeping bag in the corner under the staircase. His responsibility was handed over to me as I was his section 2IC (second in command). The main bedroom was given to the platoon commander and the Sergeant. Two Section got the living room whereas another room upstairs was allocated to Three Section.

House is always a house that gives protection from sun, rainfall, snow, frost and windy weather.

Sunday June 20 1982

Placing a mat on the floor and a sleeping bag over it, I comfortably slept, and woke up in the morning. The experience, sleeping in a house after over a month's absent, was so nice and pleasant! Just like my other comrades, I was thrilled.

We would be in a hurry for the breakfast at seven o'clock in the morning, but we had to wait so long for the turn in the only toilet available at the house, we had been living into.

The ghangher, changed into the common cookhouse, was crowded with armed soldiers. Having had the opportunity to have meals all together, I thought I was not in North Arm but in Church Crookham instead. The moment we got chance to drink tea along with eggs, doughnuts, sausages and bacons prepared by our own chef, I felt so much similarity that of the proper cook house.

Before lunch, we went to a short tour of North Arm for familiarisation. The local people, who, we met on the way, showed cordiality waving their hands. We got enough information about the settlement. Because of not having snowfall, sheep's flocks would look gorgeous on the green lawns. The weather was pleasant in the sunlight.

We ate rice, dal (lentil) and meat curry at the noon and in the evening. However, fresh vegetables were absent in the meal we had. Naturally it was impossible to get green vegetable as the weather had been adverse since our arrival in the Falklands. For weeks we hadn't had any kind of green vegetables.

Monday June 21 1982

We were allowed to purchase the limited goods in the only small shop opened for the whole settlement. Buying envelopes and letter pads were our priority because we had not written letters home. We purchased the items necessary for letters and sent home for the first time informing that the war was over and we were fit and fine. To get such opportunity to send a letter home was like winning another war. My heart was not less delighted to express long preserved feelings to my family members through letter.

I wrote a letter to my father.

Dear father,

Accept my humble honour

Respect to kanchhyama (step mother) and blessings to my junior brothers.

Presumably all of you are fine due to God's grace. I could hardly survive through your blessings and God's grace. Perhaps you heard the news of the ending of the war. The moment I was entangled in the maze of war I strongly reminisced the narrative of war you related in our childhood days. Excessive was the trouble in the battle. It was so painful. I had never seen snowfall in my life, but I saw it in the Falklands. I found the place excessively cold. The arctic clothes given to us for the battle couldn't protect us from the nasty cold.

The place is so far away from the UK. We had to take a long voyage in the ocean. You would say you had spent seven days and seven nights in the liner while going to Malaya. But the voyage to Falklands took us even twenty one days and twenty one nights. We didn't have to lose our precious lives as the enemies surrendered at the time of final attack. If otherwise happened, our life would be uncertain. Many British soldiers were killed. Argentinian enemies' casualty was so huge. Their corpses were lying everywhere unclaimed.

Now the war is over. Don't worry about me. Bhena (husband of one's sister, in this case my only elder sister's husband) is also safe and sound, too. Please let someone convey this message to my sister.

We are given order to stay for three-four months in the Falklands for its security. We have to return later as we came in the battle in the second group. Parachute Regiment, Marine and Commandos are returning soon to the UK in the first group.

I will surely come to Nepal in long leave after my return from here. If my leave was not cancelled I would be in Nepal at this time. Anyway, I will receive the medal of the war. In fact, I am very delighted.

Additionally, it might be correct what you have said to me about my marriage. Hopefully, the girl chosen to be my match by my phupu (the sister of one's father) and pusain (the husband of one's phupu) is fine. My phupu's father -in-law frequently sends me letter writing 'grandson, you ought to marry the girl I have selected for you.' We will discuss further about it after my arrival.

I have no exact idea about the money that I will have, but upon my return we shall buy land in an urban location. I think we should not buy land in the hills since you have bought enough over yonder. I am planning to purchase a piece of land in Dharan.

I will send you letter after returning to the UK. Please take care of your health. Get the brothers to concentrate on studies. Sorry for mistakes. This much for today.

Your loving son
Ganesh Rai

Father was the closest person to me. I didn't have any knowledge of mother's love as she had died when I was a child. Though I wished to write to my would-be bride, I didn't have her address. I hadn't seen her either.

Tuesday June 22 1982

In North Arm, where sheep farming and fishing were major professions like in other settlements, there was no effect of the war as Argentine troops had not been deployed there. The settlement was peaceful and secure. We were a little free from post-war activities.

We practised many kinds of military trainings in order to boost up the local residents' morale as they liked to watch us. We built assault courses from locally available materials which we improvised. There was a programme made to train and sharpen the military skills of junior ranks like us. Gurujis trained and supervised us in various aspects of military nitty gritty. Apart from the assault course, we needed to go through the orienteering and section attacks. We got involved in defence construction around the settlement for defeating enemies' in case of an assault by the Argentine forces as this was our primary task. Time table was made for assault course, attack, orienteering and so on. All ranks below Corporal, were trained by senior Corporals.

Wednesday June 23 1982

Sheep-farming was the most important industry at North Arm, just like it was for most of the Falklands Islands in those days, along with fishing in the sea. However, the people of North Arm would not eat sheep offal, but we Gurkhas loved it. So, in the heart-pinching cold of North Arm we tastily enjoyed the meal of hot rice with the fresh mutton offal curry. It was a wonderful change for the better after our lives in the cold living on military rations.

Those of us who were single (and some of us who weren't) enjoyed chatting up the local ladies.

'Hi Norma! How are you?' (Norma is not her real name but I change her name to avoid embarrassing her : North Arm is a small community.)

'Oh! Hi Dipak! Good to see you again!'

Few days earlier, Dipak and I were introduced to Norma in the shop. She invited us for tea in the next evening. We went to see her carrying chocolates. She served us sweet coffee and delicious cake. Her way to talk frankly was sweeter than the coffee she offered. A little unease, we felt due to her father's entry in the room. Fortunately, the father was as frank as the daughter.

Later on, whenever we met, Norma's father would say, 'Hi lads! How you keeping?'

We loved being friends with these excellent people whom we had helped to liberate from the invaders.

On a sunny day, we could see flocks of penguins enjoying on the beach. For us, it was not only romantic scene to see them enjoy but surprising and fortunate too. The beautiful pied penguins would hide in the water after the snowfall begins. Without leaving any trace of their existence, penguins would plunge into the sea.

Due to the snowfall in North Arm, not only ground got frozen, but a small channel of the sea froze too. For the first time in my life, I experienced not only war in the Falklands, but the snowfall as well.

Thursday June 24 1982

Ten days after the war ended, there was some terrible news. Lance Corporal Buddha Prasad Limbu and his company were busily filling in a trench dug by enemies. While he was doing so, his shovel happened to strike an unexploded M-79 grenade which was buried in the trench. There was a huge explosion in which 21161666 Lance Corporal Buddha Prasad of Signals Platoon, was killed. We got stunned to hear it. I could hardly imagine how terribly grieved his family, relatives and friends would be.

In the battlefield any message is passed on through radio sets as soon as possible. However, it's not possible for all to hear the news at once since everyone doesn't possess the radio. That's why; in the section and platoon's order, news and messages are circulated so that nobody will remain unknown about the true news. However, for the relatives and family of an individual, it takes time to get factual news about accident because adversities are more during the war-time.

On the alien soil of the thousands of miles away the light of Buddha Prasad's life departed forever. His wishes of life withered without blooming. Life is momentary. What is more to say to our co warrior Buddha Prasad in the battle field, than saying 'Farewell Comrade! Good bye!'

Tuesday June 29 1982

In course of doing various military activities, we had orienteering exercise. We had to return to the finishing point as soon as possible by reaching to the Check Points we had been assigned to. Each check points were kept quite a far distance apart. All of us ran away to find out our own Check Points with the assistance of the maps and the compasses. Although it had been snowing since last night, I didn't feel cold anymore in the slightly snow falling morning.

Exhaling out on the snow-covered open land I also kept running to reach the check points. Light snowfall change into heavy snowing. I was all alone as it was being conducted as an individual orienteering training. In some places flocks of sheep were found about to be buried by snowfall. I increased my pace of running thinking that the dense snowfall might bury me, too. On the route, I hardly met a man at the cross path.

'Hello forty-seven guruji! This snowfall troubled us much.'

I looked to the direction the sound was coming from; it was none other than Uttarhang. I said, 'Yes, yaar (a word for a close friend). This snowfall definitely created chaos.'

Both of us parted and ran towards our own Check Points.

Approximately in two hours, I came back to the finishing point completing the journey to the ascertained Check Point. Some colleagues were returning. Some already returned. My body was all sweating. Clothes needed to be washed. Anyway, a very good opportunity came to meet Norma. My heart thrilled with pleasure.

'Hey boys! Oxtail soup and tea are ready for you. You can have it. Otherwise this kind of coldness causes you pneumonia.' The platoon commander Mani Prasad Rai said. I recalled Norma's hot coffee accompanied by her profuse smile.

Dipak who was also wet with sweating, probably was thinking the same.

As our days to separate with North Arm and the entire Falklands were shortening, our company organised a mini fair with the intention of providing entertainment to the local residents. We demonstrated weaponry used in the war and their usage were also explained. Local residents participated the event enthusiastically. They thoroughly observed our exhibition and appreciated our work.

In the evening, there was a musical event held by the regimental Pipes and Drums in order to strengthen our reminiscence for future. With the ear pleasing melody of pipes and drums, we displayed march past in front of local residents. They got excited and happily accepted our display. North Arm echoed with sounds of applause.

After the march past was over, on behalf of the company, a kukri was gifted as a token of love to the Chief of the Settlement by company commander Captain Lester Holy. Though the Falklands Islanders had neither seen nor heard about the Gurkhas, their love, assistance and appreciation got imprinted in our heart. Neither purchasable nor forgettable their priceless impression permanently occupied our heart. A history of close attachment with the North Arm residents was created.

The volume of cordiality extended. The circle of friendship expanded. The amiable Falklands Islanders became our support during our stay. Our heart was not ready to move away leaving them back. Nevertheless, the alternative of separation was neither with them nor with us. No matter how much we pray to undo the day of parting, as a natural rule, it surely comes.

Thursday July 1 1982

In the first morning of the new month, delicate sun rays seen spilled over white snow. But the weather was considerably cold even though it was a sunny morning.

As usual, after the breakfast, along with tea, we involved in assault course. The assault course was set up near to the house of the local town chief. So, the town Chief organised a party at his home in honour of the command level of our company to mark the victory over the Falklands. Lower ranks were not invited to the chief's house. The personnel belonging to the lower rank like us were not involved.

We continued our assault course training till the lunch time. The hardest of all was the task of passing through the tyre in fighting order role i.e. with webbing and personal weapons. The tyre was hung about three foot off the ground with the strings. The town chief and his wife were impressed by our performance in war exercise. Also, there were the company commander, Captain Lester Holy and 2IC, Captain (QGO) Dal Bahadur Sunuwar who, were the two guests, present with town chief and his wife.

'Well done guys!' Captain Holy said, 'The chief and his wife were very much impressed with you all.'

Who doesn't get excited about being admired?

Wednesday July 7 1982

Some of us had literary duties while we were stationed on the Falklands in the aftermath of the war.

'Corporal Ram!' the platoon commander directed, 'You need to write an article in English about the battle for our magazine *Parbate*.'

The work of a soldier can embrace many disciplines, not only fighting.

I also had some literary work to do. I also began to note down the Nepalese literary pieces of my friends and my own as much as possible in the notebook bought in the local shop. Amritman excessively laughed out loud, the moment Dipak recited his jhyaure (a popular folk melody in Nepali songs and poems) poem written in parody form. The evening Dipak gulps down two cans of beer, he would incessantly flow river of his poem.

'Hey Dipak, Are you trying to be Bhanubhakta (a pioneer Nepali poet who translated the Ramayana, a great epic in Sanskrit written by Balmiki, into Nepali) but you will never be like him.' His numbery Ek Bahadur ridiculed Dipak. The day Dipak meets Norma, he sings in sentimental tone:

Timilai dekhera aankha tyahi chhadi hinde ma (I moved ahead leaving my eyes there where I saw you).

Friday July 16 1982

It was, sadly, time to leave.

It was as if darkness prevailed over the horizon of my heart because the moment of farewell from North Arm was approaching fast. Perhaps, the local people of North Arm felt the same on our departure from their settlement and darkness might tinged the local residents' firmament of heart, too.

My heart was much heavier than the heavy load I carried on my back during war. We were obliged to separate and never to meet them again. This separation was like the saying goes: 'leaving through the same door takes you to multiple journeys.'

Carrying the loads of bergen on our back, pouches strapped from the shoulder and buckled on our waist and rifle in our hands, we started pacing towards Chinook helicopter to get ourselves boarded. Norma was also present to witness this parting moment along with other local residents. They without blinking their eyes lovingly looked at our departure. They waved the hands of farewell. Their faces were pity-arousing. The teardrops oozed out of their eyes in love at the moment of valediction were much more powerful than the assault of weapons. They would violently shake and crumble the heart.

We had to fly and we flew away. We had to separate from North Arm and we separated. We flew away filling our hearts with memories enough for our whole life. We parted keeping the memories of their assistance and well-wish fresh forever.

We flew from North Arm in a Chinook helicopter. The moment we were flying with heavy heart, the local weather turned out to be dark. Due to poor visibility we became anxious of possible incident in the darkness-enveloped black firmament and amid dire sea, the anxiety of possible accident tormented us. Probably, the weather witnessed our close relation connected with North Arm. If not, why did the weather look mournful as if going to drop tears!

After a short flight, our Chinook successfully landed on the liner Uganda. We heaved a sigh of relief. Now, we left the Falklands behind.

As the process of all the companies of the battalion to arrive from their locations completed, the atmosphere turned to be interesting and cordial. The meaning of reunion with the co-warriors, who had been separated after we landed for the first time on the Falklands, was like the renewal of our mutual introduction. The UK returning atmosphere became so cordial as though we were in fact returning to our own homeland. Frankly speaking, the atmosphere was of genuinely Nepali rural style inspiring to reach home at the soonest and narrate the whole bundle of stories of the war.

'Fifty-eight numbery, how are you?' I expressed my happiness and curiosity at once when, I coincidently met numbery Hasta Bahadur Limbu of A Company at the dining hall during lunch time, whom I had not met throughout the period of war.

'I am so lucky that I am still alive.' He further clarified, 'In the night of bombardment of the Tumbledown attack I was very close to 21159185 Corporal guruji. The bombard made the Corporal half dead. God knows how I remained untouched.'

I got all surprised to hear the narrative of the numbery, who survived with his luck. For the purpose of closing the chapter of the bitter experiences of Hasta numbery, I humorously said, 'Numbery, God has saved you for your menchhima, (fascinating and mature beloved girl) isn't it?'

'Numbery, you refurbished the reminiscence of our dance in the recruitment accompanied by the song: mari gae relimai daibako kakhaima, bachunjela relimai pyariko aankhaima (if expired, on God's lap, till life goes on, on the eyes of beloved).'

'If killed in the battle we would be under the turf of the Falklands. Now it's time to join the beloved's lap, isn't it numbery?' I didn't want to make our talks intricate.

At the time of recruit training at Training Depot in Hong Kong, we were together, at the opposite beds. The letters sent by his menchhima we would read together hiding ourselves behind the cupboard door.

'And how much did your menchhima's reminiscence haunt you in the battle, numbery?'

'Oh, my goodness! numbery,' hesitatingly he said, 'Her love much troubled me when I got her letter in the liner on the same day we set off for the battle.'

'Let me act as the pageboy in your wedding ceremony, okay?' I didn't give up teasing him.

'What is the talk about, in a low volume like a couple, between you two?' Lance Corporal Ratan Bahadur was approaching us.

'Nothing special guruji,' I tried to divert the subject matter, 'Just about experiences and memory of the war.'

Chapter 10: Returning to the UK and life afterwards

Saturday July 17 1982

The sun concealed by the black clouds didn't come outside on the next day, too. I thought the furious sun didn't want to drop tears in our farewell. The external environment was joyless, desolate and dark alike.

I was excited at the prospect of returning to the United Kingdom. At twelve noon, the SS Uganda departed from the Falklands. This ship, we got onboard was kept busy on the wounded's treatment during the war period, the wounded soldiers recovered after the treatment. However, Uganda was pretty much like the wounded itself. For the last time, I wished to see the Falklands merely once. Darkness veiled my view. Why is this night like darkness in the name of day? I inwardly expressed displeasure that my wish was left unfulfilled.

I would like to express my homage for the last time to the Falklands that resurrected my life in the armed services. But my wish couldn't materialise. Protest waves were powerfully emerging within me so that it could push Uganda ashore, and I could fulfil my wishes. But so was not the case. Those feelings arose and exhausted within meaningless. My inner eyes could visualise the Falklands even though darkness veiled it. The risk we took in the Tumbledown attack kept haunting me throughout. In the similar fashion, I memorised the kind-hearted people of Goose Green and North Arm. Especially, Mr Johnson and Norma who, I would never forget in my life. Had

Mr Johnson not let us live in his house, we would have lived out on the open ground. And Norma, who would wash the dirty clothes of others and invite for a cup of coffee to strangers ?

Preserving so many layers of memories in heart, we sailed towards our destination, the Ascension Island.

There were medical staffs, our co-warriors of Sixteen Field Ambulance onboard with us too in SS Uganda. They were the people who would administer first aid and rescue the wounded in the battlefield and send them to Uganda for treatments. Our salutation to them and the humanitarian role they played during the war would be much less than their contribution. We were lucky enough and honoured to be in their company in Uganda.

Sunday July 18 1982

The welcome rise in temperature gave us the signal that we were nearing to the Ascension Island. How much would penguins rejoice in the snow-fallen cold Falklands if a palmful of heat of the parching sun we could carry from the Ascension Island? How grateful would the Falkland Islanders be? My heart merely imagined an impossible thing.

The scene of dolphin flocks vivaciously playing in the blue, clean and quiet sea looked awesome. Dolphins, that were seen following Uganda by sinking and hiding in the water as well as jumping high were pleasant. In our victorious journey perhaps, they were about to perform a welcome dance.

Naturally, the difference between going to the battlefield and returning from there winning the war, was tremendous. Many types of war trainings were practised to defeat the enemies while going to the war whereas there was not anything like that while returning. Argentines were already defeated, and we didn't have any enemy to attack immediately. The situation kept all the soldiers happy so there seemed no trace of slight anxiety appeared on their face. I wished, as others did, to reach Church Crookham (Hampshire England) as soon as possible.

Tuesday July 20 1982

All weapons including the rifles and the GPMGs were centralised and securely kept as there was no space available for armoury where all weaponry could be kept securely. Therefore, we no longer required to carry the weapons wherever we go. Though we were returning to the UK after the ending of the war, early in the morning, we were made to run on the liner's deck to keep us fit. It's not possible to control commotion and disturbance on the liner, the moment a whole battalion of soldiers run on it. The Gurkha feet caused vibration on the upper deck of the liner.

There were Indians working as laundrymen in the liner. They washed our clothes. Due to our neighbourly relationship, we got chance to eat chapati and curry together. We also got the chance to watch the Bollywood films that they would watch. I was a great fan of Amitav Bachchan. No less than that of Hema Malini as well. I was crazy about their films.

Friday July 23 1982

There was not any special work on SS Uganda after the early morning exercise of around thirty to forty minutes. The number of soldiers who play cards secretly during the time that was allocated to do personal admin, got increased. We were not allowed to play dahalmara (a kind of game in play cards) even without money for entertainment. The gamblers however, wouldn't be satisfied in dahalmar game without money. They surreptitiously organised the games of 'Marriage' and Golkhadi (a type of game in play cards). I was not fond of playing card and gambling, so I always remained away from these kinds of illegal activities. But some of the colleagues from my section immersed in cards.

We spent our time just talking and teasing to each other. During the boring moments, we would go to the deck, bask in the sun amid the fresh air and relax watching in the blue sea. The moment would be delightful. Sometimes women of 16 Field Ambulance would also appear on the deck. For the same sake, we would be thrilled to climb up the deck.

Normally, women are not sent to the frontline of the battlefield during the war, though they are soldiers. Rather they would be given other administrative responsibilities. Female soldiers in the Falklands were also dispatched in various administrative sectors. They played assistive roles like managing letters, preparing food, helping the wounded in the medical sector and so on. In the liner, along with us, female nurses who worked in Sixteen Field Ambulance also were returning to the UK. Similar to us, they would climb up the open deck for basking in the sun in order to forget the cold of the Falklands.

We would feel it was a great achievement to see the mature sexy women busy on sunbath with our lascivious eyes.

Saturday July 24 1982

Lance Corporal Ratan Bahadur, who had just returned from the company headquarters, called for a roll call to inform the order to all the members of the platoon. All of us gathered. As usual, I guessed the roll call was called for thanks giving for our disciplined bravery in the battle. Furthermore, I surmised the order would be about excellent dress and turn out or heighten the glory of Gurkhas. What could be more than this in an order?

'Don't turn a deaf ear to this,' Ratan Bahadur began to speak in warning style, 'The Commanding Officer has vehemently ordered there shouldn't be noise in the morning exercise. Apparently, complaints are made. You should run without making noise. The early morning exercise should be continued until further order.'

My expectation was that we would be ordered to get rid of early morning exercise, but it did not happen. My expectation of getting release from the morning time exercise shattered.

'This order is from the Gurkha Major,' he further said casting his eyes on the notebook, 'He has said if you are found playing cards, it will be unpardonable. Hence, none of you ought to play cards.'

That's fine. I became glad within. My anger subsided that the card-playing friends would not let me sleep throughout the night. The card-players miserably looked at each other.

'Now, let me announce another order made by the RSM (Regimental Sergeant Major).'

No sooner had Ratan Bahadur profusely smiled saying this and touching his hair than Senior Corporal Ran Bahadur teased him.

'Hey Ratne, don't smile. Everybody knows you are a maruni (a male who would dress up and wear make ups just to look alike a woman and perform the woman's role in dancing). Why do you smile untimely in front of all these guys?'

'An order is issued about hair. Hence, I smiled due to the love of hair,' Ratan Bahadur clarified.

'What's the order about hair? Let us know,' Ran Bahadur demanded.

'Nothing more. What could it be, the war is over. Now everybody should get hair trimmed. This is what the Regimental Sergeant Major has ordered.' He made things clear.

Eventually, all of us checked our heads and found the hairs grown long like of the go-go dancers.

'Who does trim our hairs? Where are the scissors, guruji?' All of us expressed indignation to Ratan Bahadur as if he was the Regimental Sergeant Major himself.

Ratan Bahadur, who did not have any clue, kept quiet.

'Neither we have barbers, nor scissors. Is the order to trim the hair is enough in itself?' After returning to the room I indignantly commented.

'Now they began meaningless Gurkha activities. Showing off your Gurkha style?' Dipak's discontent surfaced. 'The ones turned to be mice in the war now try to be tigers.'

'If you do unnecessary activities during morning exercise just to please the commander, then of course it troubled you.'

Amritman shot out his furore about the morning exercise. There does have no meaning of any lividness. You can't make any changes no matter how much you boil up. It is something like the appearing and disappearing of the huge waves in the sea. Rages are worthless in the army.

Sunday July 25 1982

Ratan Bahadur became a barber himself. Nobody knew from where he brought the scissors. The expedition of trimming the go-go style hair continued until there left no one with long hair in the platoon. After the hair cut, unknown remained no more unknown, it was prevailed that Lance Corporal Ratan Bahadur has all the attributions to be a good barber. Some of our friends had their hair trimmed by cajoling the Indian, who was employed as a laundryman in Uganda ship. The man, later on began to charge three pound per head as he saw a crowd of soldiers willing to get their hair trimmed.

Dipak, as expert as in talk, was expert in trimming the hair as well. Free of charge, he trimmed the hair of the soldiers of our section.

Wednesday July 28 1982

After almost eleven days long continuous voyage in Uganda, we reached Ascension Island. The time was seven o'clock in the morning. It was a bright and sunny morning.

We were abnormally exhausted both physically and mentally

due to the trauma caused by war and monotonous voyage in Uganda. An opportunity of playing football on the hot sand was provided to us in order to refresh our body. The pleasure of jumping, running and falling on the field, where the sunlight from the distant firmament spilled all over the sand, was transcendental. The game which we played on our own accord was capable to remind us the glory of life making us forget the nightmarish war experiences.

It was our great luck as well as coincidence to get an opportunity to sprawl and roll idly on the bosom of the desert.

We boarded the bus with the perspiring bodies covered with African sand. The bus dropped us on the side of SS Uganda.

SS Uganda, which stopped for eight hours in the searing hot Ascension Island for refuelling, again moved ahead in the world of water. Our psychology was not similar to the moment while going to the battlefield. A wretched question mark about our own life was not now suspended on our forehead at all. The frightless atmosphere gradually let our life thrill and vibrate in its original rhythm.

Thursday July 29 1982

The same circumstance, same atmosphere, a prolonged journey in water. It's hardly surprising ocean passengers get bored.

With the purpose of keeping soldiers active and engage in sporting event, inter-company water polo competition was organised in the swimming pool of SS Uganda. This water polo game much refreshed the disheartened psyche of the soldiers who were recently released from the cruel shadow of war in the

Falklands. I was a good swimmer, so I was chosen to represent my company, B Company. But never had any experience of a game like water polo previously. Seven of us teamed up together and had a few sessions of training before the competition. In the first round we beat C Company and progressed to another round, where we got beaten by Headquarter Company. That was end of the competition for us.

We had been viewing the magical romance of penguin in the Falklands and dolphins' dance in the voyage. In course of time, we transformed into penguin and dolphin to plunge into the swimming pool.

Friday July 30 1982

There was another entertainment event organised in the Theatre Hall, which had never witnessed the tom-tom melody. It not only enjoyed tom-tom melody but also flexibly bent its waist in maruni (a popular type of Nepalese folk dance) dance. Throughout the hall, people began to dance in maruni steps. Rifleman Mahendra Rai, a popular maruni in the whole battalion, dressed up to be a female and performed his wonderful dance. There were other single, duet and group dances as well but none matched the popular Mahendra's dancing talent.

The entire audiences were mesmerised when the soldiers, glistening the lightning like sharp knife, performed kukri dance.

The great round of applause for the dance was much more clamorous than the two-way firing in the Tumbledown onslaught.

Saturday July 31 1982

What is more worth doing than fun and entertainment in the ephemeral human life! Our military life deprived of fun and entertainment would usually gather in the evening on the open deck of Uganda in order to dance bending our waist flexibly. We would forget ourselves in the funny atmosphere of dancing, singing and jokes. War memories would radically disappear from our memory too.

Meanwhile, the evening happened to be a memorable one as the song sang by extremely shy Amritman, who is in our section and is considerably mature in age but a bit junior in recruitment, made the whole platoon burst into laughter. He made us laugh so much that it resulted in the saturation of laughter in military life. He had sung a popular folk song:

Hatai katyo palise churale
Maya phatyo gaungharko kurale
Purba bagne Gandaki hai, paschim bagne Bheri
Timro hamro mayapriti bhet hunchha ki pheri
Hatai katyo…

(Polished bangle hurt my hand
Village rumours ruptured our love
Eastward-flowing Gandaki, (one of the three biggest
rivers in Nepal that flows through the middle part of the
country) westward-flowing Bheri (another big river in
western Nepal.)
Possibly our love joins once more)

While singing 'eastward-flowing Gandaki' as per the song's melody he would turn the face eastward and while singing 'westward-flowing Bheri' he would turn the face westward. His physical gesture and gravity of the vocal made us burst into laughter. I laughed out loud with my eyes full of tears. I thought I would never forget this moment and especially the way how Amritman sang and acted according to the sentiment of the song.

Then after, our colleagues got a very strong issue to tease Amritman. They laughed at him singing the song 'eastward-flowing Gandaki' 'westward-flowing Bheri' by turning their heads as per the direction. In response, Amritman, a composed individual would just keep grinning.

Sunday August 1 1982

In course of our return to UK after winning the war in the Falklands, we had wonderful news as rewards, promotion orders were made in SS Uganda. Already excited with victory, the ones who received the steeple of promotion on their heads got overwhelmed with pride.

Our platoon commander, Warrant Officer Mani Prasad Rai, who would always raise our morale high saying 'don't worry Four Platoon, I will bring you back home safe and sound from the battleground,' got promoted in the post of the Lieutenant (QGO). Similarly, five Platoon commander Lieutenant (QGO) Bhuwani Shankhar Rai, also got promoted in the post of the Captain (QGO) and now would wear three stars studded rank badge on his shoulder. Their promotion brought happiness among us. We, being the rank of Riflemen, though much dominated in the prospect of promotion, were more thrilled than them in our platoon commanders' promotion.

In our titillation there was definitely happiness and more than that it contained an indirect request for our own welfare i.e. my own promotion as I was competent enough to be a Lance Corporal, who had been a section 2IC (Second in Command) throughout the war.

The more SS Uganda was nearing to Southampton Port, the more I thought we were approaching home as if somebody was desperately waiting for welcoming us or a sense of imagination filled my heart as if I was in a hurry to see someone very close to my heart as soon as possible. In fact, there was no near and dear one of ours in the empty Barracks. Neither parents, nor brothers, nor sister nor any close relatives. Eventually, no one at all. Merely a memory. Merely a figment of imagination. Nothing more than just a memory and imagination. How unlucky soldiers we were that we didn't have anyone to share our happiness, our survival and of course our sorrow! What a cruel compulsion to tie up the experiences of our contentment and misery inside our heart and not finding anyone to share with.

Monday August 9 1982

And so, after about three months, SS Uganda brought us back to the same port exactly at eleven o'clock in the morning, from where QE II had got us to set off towards the Falklands for the battle.

What a tremendous contradiction between departing and arriving!

The hearts disheartened in our departure were pumped up in our arrival. Prior to our arrival to Southampton, there were small boats with elated people, hurriedly came to welcome us. We saw the port, filled with polychromatic crowd of hundreds of people, from afar.

I wished to reach the port as soon as possible and see all the dear ones who were eagerly waiting for our reunion. In the unexpected happy reunion, my heart one-sidedly wished to embrace with the dear ones and let two drops of tear fall down.

The more SS Uganda was nearing to the port, the more the crowd's exhilaration mounted. As Uganda was going to stop, people in the crowd with banners, posters and play cards that they were holding, began to rise and wave forcibly. The process continued until the liner stopped. The more our arrival was nearing to the port, the more the exciting activities and echoes of the cheering crowd rolled up. Consequently, the atmosphere of the port grew alluring.

When nerve-tickling music began to ring in our ears I felt like wading through the illimitable flood of happiness. We all warriors, rejoicing our victory on the open deck of Uganda, stood in shoulder to shoulder in order to accept the honour offered by the crowd. At that moment our thrilled heart didn't like to be imprisoned within the volume of ribs.

Eventually, Uganda docked in Southampton harbour. The atmosphere filled with the joy of the piercing shriek of the crowd, blasting, clapping and waving their jubilant hands above their heads. Happiness multiplied when the shrill siren of the liner mixed. Waves of cheerfulness expanded far and wide.

WELL DONE
WELCOME HOME
WE ARE PROUD OF YOU -
AAYO GURKHALI ! (here come the Gurkhas).

Our delight crossed the boundary to see the harbourage embossed with the play cards and banners containing the aforementioned and many more messages. From the deck, I saw Field Martial Sir Edwin Bramall and regimental Colonel of 7th DEO Gurkha Rifles Brigadier E. D. Smith were already present to welcome us the Gurkhas. My joy increased two times more.

Saying goodbye to SS Uganda's crews, we disembarked the liner carrying our belongings like bergens, pouches and personal weapons. We had only just boarded off the SS Uganda, an insuperable crowd surrounded us. As we were addressed with honorific phrases and metaphors by public I thought we had done something worth praising for.

Some people patted us, and many people embraced and lovingly touched our cheeks. Furthermore, some women kissed on our cheeks. Those kisses were not inspired by carnal desires. That was purely their compliments to us for what we had done for their nation. It was a genuine evaluation of our unmatchable dedication keeping life at risk for the glory and prestige of the British people. The moment, filled with honour and appreciation, was risen high from the filthy swamp of segregation. Perhaps humanity was amused at that moment.

Following the open track made by the police in the middle of the crowd, we entered a huge custom house. Returned from the battleground, we didn't have anything else except arms, ammunitions and war experiences for custom checking. If we had something it was just invisible wound hidden inside the bosom. Gurkha blood was flowing in veins.

We were not obstructed in the custom office for any checks. We moved towards the coaches that were waiting for us and boarded them. Our journey to Fleet Town began, which was about two hours long.

While we were on the move on wide motor way, people from inside the glass windows of cars and buses were giving us thumbs up and waving hands. Such responses of British people made me forget adversities of war and risks I faced. The struggle I had been through during the battle also vanished. Human life seems to be born to get excited in compliments.

We stopped at the Fleet Town Railway Station that was near our Church Crookham Barracks. The crowd of local residents, who were pre-informed about our return, did welcome us at the place where our coaches stopped. The atmosphere around would articulate that the meaning to be winner is to find oneself in the series of welcome and honour.

Following the company roll number, we stood in three files on the road readied for the march past. In the sonorous melody of pipes and drums and maintaining the rhythm of steps, we moved ahead holding our head high by covering the entire road. Hundreds of residents of Fleet and surrounding areas gave us company with a big hand, waved flags and cheered us. They also exposed the banners and play cards written 'Johnny Gurkha.' I came to realise that the welcome ceremony organised by residents of Fleet was much more immense than that of Southampton Port.

There was Field Martial Sir Edwin Bramall along with Mr George Watson, the Councillor of Fleet Town, stood on the saluting dais that was in the middle part of the town. The reason they were in the dais was to receive the honour offered by the officers and other ranks of the First Battalion, Seventh DEO Gurkha Rifles who caused victory of the British army in the Falklands war.

After crossing Fleet Town through the march past, we waited on queue to board the coaches on the football ground. I wished to walk in the same way up to nearby Church Crookham Barracks. However, a junior soldier's wish is just a wish nothing more than that.

The reason behind the grand welcome to our return by the public in Fleet, was that we had heightened their glory by directly representing them in the war and recapturing the Falklands. Furthermore, it was our local area and there were some acquaintances. Hence, I wished this victory procession continued on foot up to the camp. Ironically, everything doesn't happen in life exactly in the format we think or wish. We boarded the coaches and headed for the camp.

The time was five o'clock in the afternoon and the sunlight was pleasant. It felt as warm as mother's lap. At some places along the road, I saw few local residents welcoming and encouraging us by waving union jacks and our regimental bunting flags. My eyes suddenly fell upon a gentle woman waving the national flag of my country Nepal in one hand and a play card in other hand that read: 'WELCOME HOME, BRAVE GURKHAS' while the coach I was on was about to reach the Wyvern pub in the corner near the camp. My heart was overwhelmed with joy when I saw the lady flying my national flag and welcoming me in a foreign land. It was absolutely a profound honour to have seen this lady in such way. I wished the woman was my own mother.

The Queen Elizabeth II Barrack, I guessed, was energised with our entrance through the main gate. Its energisation was like that of a delighted mother who hurriedly runs to get her children as fast as she can who just returned after many years in foreign land and hugs them tight. The empty barracks did welcome me as if a candle of happiness was just ignited.

I grew glad as well as sentimental for which I enjoyed the warm embrace of the mother-like barrack. Unknowingly my eyes got teary in the happiness of reunion as though I forgot myself or I searched myself in the depth of feeling. Maybe it is the reason that a tremendous love, faith and honour grows for life.

Sunday August 15 1982

The civilian staff of the camp and the local people organised a fair on the green lawn in front of the battalion Headquarter and Guardroom. There was no reason for not attending the fair because it was organised for our honour. Moreover, an order was issued to attend the fair. Items such as clothes, foods and sporting goods were displayed for sale at various stalls. There were beautiful young girls at every stall to entice the soldiers' heart and make a good profit.

We were made to wear regimental mufti with blazer and tie. The civilians talked with us mostly about the war and our feelings. Considerable was the presence of the retired officers who had worked with Gurkhas especially in far east; Borneo, Malaya, Singapore, Hong Kong, Burma etc.

'Ram Ram hajur! (the old fashioned but polite way of greeting in Nepali language) Kasto chha tapainlai?' (How are you?') Speaking in Nepali, a retired Gurkha officer came to me for handshake.

'Ma thik chuu hajur,' (I'm fine sir). I replied and asked him about the Gurkha regiment he had served with.

'I was in First Battalion, Tenth Gurkha Rifles.' He showed the medal on his bosom and said, 'Fought Borneo War and received the medal.'

I thought that I was going to receive a medal, too. I recalled the South Atlantic medal that was getting prepared in the factory. Once I received the medal how proud I would be.

'Guys! One pound each,' a young and attractive woman displaying a vest spoke, 'It's for charity.'

I thought to buy one if it was for charity. More than that, how could I ignore an offer made by a sexy woman like her? Every one of us in our group bought a vest each in order to recall our memories of both the fair and the young lady as well. I returned to the barrack with Dipak and Amritman at the time the fair was almost over.

Tuesday August 17 1982

A notice was issued in the afternoon that the whole battalion were to stand down for two weeks block leave. We could go even to Nepal for a month long leave however, the airfare had to be managed by the individual concerned. Having had served almost three years, I was due for my first six months long leave to Nepal. So, I did not think it was a good idea to fly out to my home country and increase the expenditure anyway. I planned to visit London, so I forwarded my name to the platoon Sergeant.

Friday August 20 1982

Britain and the British people were still seemed to be over the moon after successfully recapturing the Falklands Islands. Television channels had been continuously broadcasting footages about the Falklands war. The same glory of victory had been still kept flooding the newspapers' pages.

People talked about the same in the nearby towns like Aldershot and Fleet. That was very obvious as Aldershot was the home of British Army and Fleet, the neighbouring town of Church Crookham, where my regiment was based.

'Hi Johnny!' In the afternoon, I was at the Aldershot Town Centre, somebody called me from the back, 'Had you been to the Falklands?'

He was a soldier of the Parachute regiment. I asked, 'Had you been there, too?'

'Fortunately, not!' said someone, who belonged to the One Parachute regiment.

Sunday August 29 1982

Those who opted to fly to be with their loved ones, flew for Nepal for a month's leave. The photographs in addition to the news of their return to homeland were published in the British newspaper especially in the tabloids. When I saw the photos of theirs, in the front pages of the newspapers, of 'the Falklands heroes' adorned in the three pieces suits and about to board the plane at Heathrow airport, I had a kind of regret arose within me on my decision of not going home on a month block leave.

A large group of around fifty to sixty people went to Scarborough, a beautiful city in the north east England, in order to enjoy an invitation. A week-long tour with full board and lodging in a hotel for the entire group was sponsored by the local community. I regarded myself unfortunate of not being selected and enjoy the local people's warm hospitality. I just blamed my luck and waited to count the days to go to London.

'We are the most unfortunate ones,' Dipak complained his luck, 'Only the people who could speak English were told they would be taken, but there are some who are very poor in English, are taken to Scarborough, too.'

'Have patience, Dipak. The world is like that,' I tried to convince him, 'Nowhere in this world the selection process is based on fairness, that completely would follow the criteria.'

'What if only the English-speaking people went to Scarborough?' I further gave Dipak an example to convince him, 'Would this mean the ones who could not speak the language did not fight the war in the Falklands?'

Dipak kept quiet, so I guessed he got the point.

Tuesday September 14 1982

Finally, our block leave came to an end. All soldiers holiday-ing in various places - I had spent some very pleasant days in London - came back to the barrack, except those who had been to Nepal.

Sunday September 19 1982

Following the victory in the Falklands, the morale of our battalion, First Seven Gurkha Rifles's image had been boosted enormously. People did appreciate us wherever we went. The noticeboard got saturated by congratulatory letters. Upon the battalion's return from the war, the Commanding Officer and the company commanders had been busy; sometimes with journalist, sometimes chairing the meetings, attend-ing lunch meetings and so on. Receiving compliments and appreciation letters were one thing but attending every public event invited for was different thing. Because we had a very compact schedule.

The group that went to attend an invitation to Fareham in the evening was comprised of fourteen soldiers. And I was also included in the group. Fareham town, which is located in the distant south near Portsmouth, took us almost two hours by road to get there. The group commander was Assistant Education Officer, Lieutenant (QGO) Man Bir Limbu.

After a two hours long drive, we got to the wonderful town of Fareham. The congregated locals did warmly welcome us. A text was pasted on the entrance- WE WELCOME YOU

BRAVE GURKHAS. We were absolutely delighted.

Drinks were served along with snacks. In the gathering, the presence of the middle-aged was considerably more than that of senior citizens. Teenagers were comparatively less. Most of the old men were ex-army and majority of them had served in Gurkha regiments. Those old men nostalgically recalled their bygone days; especially they narrated about the wars in Borneo and Burma. They earnestly talked with us about the Falklands war. The atmosphere came to be much too bonhomous and delightsome as well.

Prior to dinner, on behalf of the community, a veteran delivered a speech, 'Gurkhas have involved in every war this country fought. And the latest one was in the Falklands…'

Through applause and cheers it was proven that his speech about war and Gurkhas' involvement in it could win everyone's heart. He handed over the microphone to Lieutenant (QGO) Man Bir Limbu for a speech.

Man Bir delivered an impressive speech in response. He related an account of Gurkha life connecting rural life to the battleground. He also expressed gratitude to the community and its associates for inviting and honouring us.

The program hall echoed with the clapping.

As soon as the dinner session was done, then they requested us, like in most places, to dance. We had carried a madal (a kind of nepali drum) along with us. The driver brought it from the vehicle. He played it and a jhyaure (a popular folk melody in Nepali songs and poems) melody began to ring in the hall:

Khuttama nail pare parla
Jhyaurema nanachi chhod dina

Nanache nache jhai gara
Markela barule kamara…

(No matter if a nail pricks my feet
I don't stop without dancing in jhyaure
Though not dancing, do like dancing
And slender waist will flexibly move…)

I spent time doing Nepalese folk dancing - something I very much enjoy - with Mahendra Rai, an expert in Nepalese folk dance. The local men and women were surprised to see us danced the way we did the sitting and standing moves. We asked them to join us for the dance. Some of them joined us and made them dance, too. They enjoyed it a lot. We made them dance until they dripped with sweat.

After the dance, it was time to say our goodbyes, which we did and then parted our ways. When we returned to the camp around midnight, the light was already out in the camp and everyone was already in their beds.

Wednesday September 22 1982

At the time of roll call by the Company Sergeant Major (CSM), it was informed that a victory parade was going to be organised in London.

I was also lucky enough to be selected to take part in victory parade.

Friday October 1 1982

After breakfast, we left QE II Barracks for Aldershot Military Garrison by Four Tone TCV (Troops Carrying Vehicle) for parade rehearsal. After reaching the assembly area for rehearsal, we were informed that senior officers of our battalion were also participating the parade. Those senior officers were; Commanding Officer Lieutenant Colonel David Morgan, Gurkha Major, Major (QGO) Lal Bahadur Rai and Captain (QGO) Khile Rai. Participants from other Infantry regiments also gathered for rehearsal. Just like ours, they had their senior officers also present.

A briefing was made before the rehearsal about what was to be done in the parade and how long the march past would take place. Then we had a walk through talk through first and followed by the proper rehearsal. We rehearsed for few more times and stopped. We returned to our camp so did the others too.

Tuesday October 5 1982

'First Battalion, Seven Gurkha Rifles, eyes left!'

As per the order, we, at once, turned our head to the left and saluted the VVIPs (Very Very Important Persons).

'As the VVIPs will be up on the balcony,' Captain (QGO) Khile directed us in a shrill voice, 'All of you should look upward and make your eyes contact with the VVIPs.'

How much up do the VVIPs take their seat? Nobody had any clue. Therefore, there prevailed confusion among us during the rehearsal. The parade ground was surrounded by oak tree lines all around. Captain (QGO) Khile said pointing to the line of the oak trees standing on the left side of the parade ground, 'Right now, look on the top of the tree.'

Throughout the rehearsal period, the top of the oak tree became Prime Minister Margaret Thatcher's eyes to me. Furthermore, whenever and wherever I saw an oak tree I assumed it as a VIP, which haunted me for some time.

Wednesday October 8 1982

I received the Falklands war medal that was named 'South Atlantic Medal' from the Quarter Master store. As you will no doubt guess, I was just so very glad and proud to receive it. On one side, Queen Elizabeth's head is imprinted along with a diadem; on the other side, the whole body of a sheep.

Somehow, the medal is deeply symbolic of the Falkland Islands, what they are and what they mean. Despite the many occasions during my time on the Falklands when I was scared of dying and extremely uncomfortable physically, I loved my time on Falklands, and I hope one day to return in a civilian capacity.

Epilogue: the Victory Parade

Tuesday October 12 1982

We made our journey to London early in the morning by coach. The assembly place for all participants was an open field near Armoury House, where we all gathered. The time was ten o'clock and the weather was not too bad. I became boundlessly happy to see the fellow soldiers representing various regiments to take part in the felicitation and victory celebration organised by the city of London. Participants from different regiments had dressed its own regimental conventional military attire. Which I found colourful and attracting.

No sooner had the watch struck 12:25 noon then the atmosphere echoed with the sonorous melody of the band of the musical instruments. Following the roll of marching order and the timing, the regiment of triumphant soldiers moved ahead synchronising footsteps. Insuperable crowd of people had gathered on both sides of the clean and wide road in London while the triumphant footsteps were treading on. The multitude of people would give such an impression as if none of the Londoners were inside their houses. The massive crowd seemed like all the Londoners were brought out by the roadside by this exciting environment.

The people had Union Jacks in the hands which they were waving and most of them had their faces tinged with the same flag's colour. This spontaneous overflow of people proved that in victory, first of all, people would remember their entire nation. The metropolitan atmosphere turned to be joyous after the clapping, cheering and flags waving of the victory-intoxicated people which echoed on the great mansions. This pattern of immense welcome and felicitation was not limited only on the roadside, but it spread out everywhere on the balconies and windows of immense buildings.

Those metropolitan mansions and buildings got covered with the Union Jacks seemed like as if their characteristic was to put on the national flags for national unity on historical occasions such as this. The way the atmosphere created by performing nationality through multi-coloured flags on the road in London was affecting the whole UK as if the Falklands war had sewed the tattered hearts and brought the whole nation together.

On both sides of the road, the London police was controlling the throng of Londoners. Otherwise overwhelmed with powerful feelings and emotions, they might come to the road to talk with us, to listen to our war narratives and to express intense love, honour and esteem to us. Perhaps they would follow our footsteps. The British were already reputed worldwide to act whimsically; if situation favoured they possibly wouldn't stay passive on such fertile occasion of victory ceremony.

We continued the marchpast shortening the rood distance. Our bosom was embellished with the scintillating South Atlantic Medal, a symbol of victory. The participants in this parade were regarded the fortunate ones to wear the Falklands War Medal. In this sense, I became like the steeple of pride on the tower of good luck.

As every coin contains two different sides, military life is no different at all as it also contains different dimensions. Though objectives, needs and interests might vary, the foremost duty of a soldier after joining military service eventually is to fight a battle. Once you are recruited in the army, you are always in the possibility of becoming a target of bullet. Gaining war experience and defeating the enemies, being involved in the battle and wearing a shining war medal on the bosom, is the ultimate aim and the only destination of military life. If these conditions are fulfilled, principally, military life is regarded worthy. That was what I conclude the military life.

In this sense, while marching on the middle of the road in London wearing a splendid and resplendent war medal, how much pride of being a soldier I felt. Even more than that I indulged in self-glorification that I honestly and successfully carried out military duty. Probably, my co-warriors did feel the same experience.

A throng of helicopters flew past above us in the sky during our march past, as if they accepted the felicitation offered by the city of London and its people. There were roars of the tanks at the rear captivating crowds' attention. Tanks were also got involved in the battle in Falklands and came out to be very useful and effective.

The great esteem, honour, and cordiality expressed by the mass standing on both sides of the road were wonderful and unimagined to me. The greatest fortune for me was to return safe and sound from the battleground without getting wounded by the enemies' bullet. It was the greatest gift of life to any soldier. I was content with it. I realised something significant I had done, when British public honoured and appreciated our bravery and triumph.

If I could see even intermittently our triangular-shaped flag consisting of the sun and the moon in the middle of the pied Union Jack waving here and there everywhere, my heart perhaps would be as high as Chomolungma (the Kirati name for Mount Everest, that is equally used in Nepal too) and bosom as wide as the plain Terai (lowland areas in the foothills of the Himalayas) with delight, self-honour and satisfaction. But I had had no chance for that great luck. When you hurriedly enter your house to narrate good news to your mother but you don't find her by the fireplace and disappointment engulfs you. Similar kind of agony bitterly pinched my heart.

The process of treading on the kumbhakarna (a mythological character in Hindu religion who used to sleep continuous for long time) like sprawling road by our military footsteps continued. After crossing almost three-quarter part of the road, I saw Mansion house on the left hand side of the road. There were the VVIPs standing on the open terrace of the huge Mansion House. The VIPs included the Prime Minister Margaret Thatcher and the Lord Mayor of the London Metropolitan. We had had enough training during the rehearsal so we smartly and in steady pace moved ahead. On the order of 'Eyes Left' by the Commanding Officer, we smartly turned our heads together to our left to offer our salute to the Prime Minister. Even though, I was continued on the move I saw the Iron Lady's face glowed with the conceit of victory much brighter than the ever-glowing sunlight in the Ascension Island. Her glory amplified after the triumph over the Falklands. As soon as our eyes contact to her eyes became no more possible we returned our heads to the front on the command of 'Eyes Front.' And we continued our march past on the broad road with the music of our own regimental Pipes regiment Drums.

I was so much thrilled and mesmerised by the Londoners' cordial honour and the respectful thundering of the clapping.

I wished the felicitation ceremony would continue incessantly in the similar fashion for three days and three nights so that I could be the focal point of their immense praise and spread in their heart. The unexhausted footsteps emboldened by happiness, glory and gladness became more excited to move ahead. I was unaware of the time until I saw Guildhall in close proximity, that was the finishing point of the marching.

Oh! How fast the half hour went!

The Guildhall, situated in the heart of the City of London, maintaining its distinct identity, was magnificent with historical arts. When the march past was over, all of us moved to the entrance to get inside the Guildhall. There were young women and pretty girls at the entrance doors to give a warm reception. Having given our names, they ushered us to the tables.

Our names were set in small cards on the round table. My seat was in between the seats of an Army General and a member of the London Metropolitan. Although there were few of my colleagues on the table, I felt a kind of discomfort within me. I took my seat and kept quiet even the seats on both sides were unoccupied. I felt a wonderful sense of equality at the prospect of such eminent people being about to sit next to me!

As those two high-profile personnel took their seats, they introduced themselves and shook everyone's hand. Immediately after their introduction they talked about the same hot cake like topic of the Falklands war. I thought they were smart enough to make my life a bit comfortable. I somehow managed to explain my experiences to them. They intently listened to my narrative.

'Did you have to sharpen your kukri too?'

It was the General who asked me this question. I said the war had turned out to be too short for that to be necessary, and that in any case, as we were moving ahead to begin our assault, the enemy fled in fear and the war ended.

An announcement was then made through the microphone that the Prime Minister, Mrs Thatcher, along with the Lord Mayor of the City of London were about to enter the Guildhall. All of us inside the hall got up in honour of those respectable personalities. The noisy hall suddenly changed into pin-drop silence. After their entry the atmosphere of the hall entirely differed. The programme turned to formality from informality.

Delicious food was brought to our table by beautiful ladies. Our empty glasses were filled with wine. I forgot the entire pains, hardships, fear and fright of the war while tasting the delicious food, enjoying the speeches and casting an oblique glance on the beauties out of the corner of my eyes. I suppose, those gorgeous ladies were brought over just to make us forget the war trauma.

There came the girls again with dessert, tea and coffee. I was not a fan of tea myself, so I had coffee with milk instead. My heart secretly wished their frequent attendance.

As soon as our meal session was over, instantly, there was a round of toast offering program in honour of the Queen Elizabeth II, British people and Task Force respectively. Once more the girls attended us and offered glasses full of champagne for toast. On the leadership of the toastmaster, we raised the glasses to offer toast and drank the champagne that repeated three times. As the segment ended, likewise ended the champagne and the empty glasses were left on the tables.

Then it was the time to deliver speeches. Mrs Margaret Thatcher was known for her toughness, that was probably why she was addressed as Iron Lady. She delivered a very strong speech. She congratulated all those people who got involved directly or indirectly in the war. And congratulated the Task Force for their sacrifice in the war in the Falklands. The Task Force resurrected the British Imperialism alive making the Falklands free from the Argentine clutch.

The Guildhall was filled with joy and excitement the moment dignitaries' applause mixed with the Prime Minister's welcome and congratulation. The way how the Prime Minister welcomed and offered her congratulations to the all soldiers who involved in Falklands war made us as if we, the members of Task Force submerged in the sea of flowery discourse forgetting the immediate reality and ourselves. Intoxicated with victory, at the moment, our hearts were overflowed with delight.

I realised, in war, there is neither wholly triumph of life nor wholly defeat of death. Contrary to it, defeat of life and triumph of death is another reality, that I experienced. The balance between life and death perhaps, depends on triumph and defeat.

We ached when Mrs Thatcher expressed heart-touching emotive words of condolence in honour and memory of those valorous warriors who were martyred while dauntlessly fighting in the battleground.

Ultimately, it is the heart that breaks into fissures when notches are cut on the knife of sentiment, no matter how much iron-like we try to make our hearts. We listened to the speech with the wounded heart that was enormously aching. All of us earnestly recalled our buddies whose physical body we wouldn't retrieve anymore. The narrative of their sacrifice is sure to be written in golden letters in history. Even though their bodies dissolve in soil, their gallantry, heroism and sacrifice will never be forgotten.

As the British say, in the words of the British poet Robert Laurence Binyon (1869-1943)

They shall grow not old, as we that are left grow old:
Age shall not weary them, nor the years condemn.
At the going down of the sun and in the morning

We will remember them.
In our language we say this of the war dead:

Jo ladaima gaye
Tara kahile ghar pharkiyenan
Tiniharulai hami
Sadhai samjhirahanechhau.

which means:

Those who went to the war and never returned home.
We will always remember them:

After the victory in the Falklands, Gurkha soldiers were praised once again for their utmost bravery and loyalty. Upon our arrival to England from the Falklands we received letters of invitation and appreciation from different parts of the country.

Fortunately, I was one of the few to get involved in many events that were organised for our honours. The local residents, whom we met, were extremely eager to know about the battle and the Gurkhas as well. Despite their considerable knowledge about Gurkhas, we found they didn't usually know about the etymological meaning of the word 'Gurkha'. They had understood the word 'Gurkha' as synonymous with courageousness, bravery and fearlessness. That may not be the precise etymology, but I am happy and proud for them to make that link in their minds with my brave people.

THE END

Also Available from The Conrad Press
Diary of a Guerilla Girl
by Tara Rai

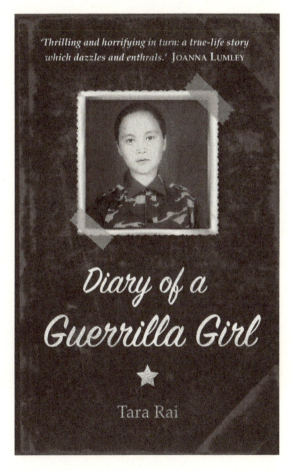

In paperback: ISBN 978-1-911546-25-2
and ebook: ISBN 978-1-912317-65-3